USBORNE

UNDERSTANDING
CLIMATE CHANGE

Written by
Andy Prentice and Eddie Reynolds

Illustrated by
El Primo Ramón

Climate Change experts:
Dr. Steve Smith and Dr. Ajay Gambhir

Designed by Jamie Ball and Freya Harrison

Contents

Chapter 4: What's stopping us?

If we know what we need to do, why aren't we already making those changes? Some of it is about getting big groups of people to agree on which changes are the most important, and some of it is to do with what's going on in our own brains.

Chapter 5: What can I do?

One person can't fix the crisis alone. But there are a lot of things that individual people CAN do, no matter how old or young, or how much power they have.

Usborne Quicklinks

For links to websites where you can find out more about the climate crisis, how it happened and how people are trying to repair the damage, go to **usborne.com/Quicklinks** and type in the title of this book.

Please follow the internet safety guidelines at Usborne Quicklinks. Children should be supervised online.

What is the climate?

Climate is often shorthand for the Earth's **climate system** – an interconnected, always-moving, insanely complicated system made up of all the air, sea, ice, land, plants and animals, interacting together.

The climate is NOT the same as the weather.

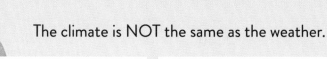

Weather is the temperature, rain and wind at a given time and place. It can change hour by hour and day to day.

Climate is what we expect the weather to be like in the long term. It changes slowly, over many decades.

Sept. 2040
28°C
82.5°F

Sept. 2030
25°C
77°F

Sept. 2020
24°C
75°F

The Earth's climate system is divided up into many different, smaller climates around the world.

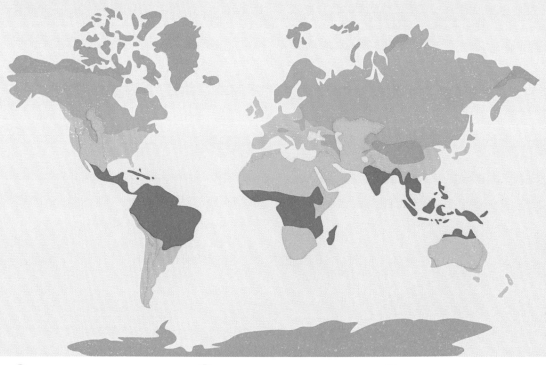

● **Polar** – Consistent cold temperatures throughout the year

● **Temperate** – Mild annual temperatures

● **Tropical** – Constant warm temperatures

● **Dry** – Not much rainfall

● **Continental** – Hot summers and cold winters

A change, or a *crisis*?

The Earth's climate is changing. To put it simply, it's getting hotter.
This **global heating** is changing our planet, putting people and nature at risk.
The change is such a huge threat, it has become a *crisis*.

Because the climate changes very slowly and weather varies day to day, it's hard to recognize that global heating is happening RIGHT NOW.

But there is no doubt that the climate *is* changing.

Things may not seem so bad NOW, but if we don't do anything to stop what's happening, the consequences will be much worse in the future.

This is why it's a CRISIS.

The good news is that there are many things we can still do to fix the crisis.
The bad news is that it's a BIG challenge to get everyone to work together.

How important is the crisis?

Not everyone agrees about this. This book is here to help you make up your own mind. Here are some examples of things different people say.

Some people need no convincing.

Other people might have heard of the climate crisis, but don't know or don't care about what they can do.

Other people deny there's a crisis at all.

Dad

The Earth's climate is always changing – I listened to a podcast about it yesterday.

Look around you! There are hot days and cold days, and there always have been. I don't think we have anything to worry about.

Crisis? *What* crisis?

To be perfectly honest, the authors of this book agree (more or less) with Dani. But, in order to solve the climate crisis, a lot of people will need to be convinced the threat is important enough to change their habits. This won't be easy.

The word 'crisis' comes from the Greek word *krisis,* which means 'a choice'. We are all going to have to make *hard choices* as we face the crisis.

Should I have a shower or a bath?

Is it ok to buy a new phone every year?

Should we make businesses pay for their pollution?

Some will be personal choices that we make for ourselves, big and small.

Other choices will affect entire countries. We will have to make these together with everyone else.

Should I have another child?

Should we ban diesel-burning cars?

Should rich countries help poorer countries invest in clean energy?

The only way to know that YOU'RE making good choices, is to make sure you *really* understand what's going on.

Chapter 1:
The basics

If the climate crisis were simple, it would be simple to fix. But it isn't. It's big, complex and hard to get your head around. Before anyone – including *you* – can choose what to do, they have to *understand* what's going on.

Our climate

Humans have existed for 200,000 years. That's *really* not that long. If you squeezed all of Earth's history into one day, we would only show up in the last four seconds. A lot happened on Earth before then.

> The current climate feels normal to us. But if you research the distant past – which scientists called paleoclimatologists do – you'll see that there's no such thing as a *normal* climate.

DESTINATION: 4.3 billion years ago

> Let's go exploring!

There have been climates so hostile, no life could survive. For the first half a billion years, the planet's surface was around 200°C (392°F).

> Don't go outside! It's far too hot.

> Animals and plants need the gas **oxygen** to survive. Back then, there was no oxygen, and no life anywhere.

4.6 billion ⟷ 4 billion years ago

There have been periods where Earth was covered almost entirely in ice...

> Whoops!

720 million ⟷ 630 million years ago

...and periods where there was little to no ice at all.

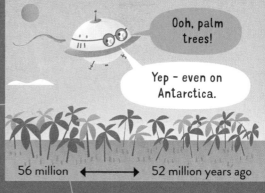

> Ooh, palm trees!

> Yep – even on Antarctica.

56 million ⟷ 52 million years ago

The thing that makes the Earth get hotter and colder is also the thing that makes life on our planet possible – *the atmosphere*. This is a thin blanket of air between the ground and outer space.

We need gases such as oxygen in the atmosphere so we can breathe.

But we also need other gases, known as GREENHOUSE GASES. They keep our planet at *just* the right temperature for life to exist.

Here's how greenhouse gases work:

1 ENERGY from the Sun HITS the atmosphere.

2 About one third of the energy is REFLECTED BACK into space by clouds or the land.

3 The other two thirds HEATS the land, sea and atmosphere.

4 Some heat ESCAPES BACK into space...

5 ...but greenhouse gases prevent some of that heat from escaping. This keeps the Earth warmer than it would be without them.

This final stage of warming is known as the **GREENHOUSE EFFECT**. Without it, we'd freeze.

Carbon dioxide

There are quite a few different greenhouse gases, but one is particularly important to explain the climate crisis: **carbon dioxide**, or **CO_2**. Adding CO_2 to the atmosphere makes the greenhouse effect stronger.

CO_2 is *emitted* into the atmosphere by some things, and *absorbed* by others.

All animals, plants and tiny lifeforms called microbes emit CO_2 in a process called **respiration**.

Plants absorb CO_2 from the air to live and grow.

Animals respire when they breathe.

Some types of soil absorb and trap lots of CO_2.

Lots of CO_2 in the air ends up being absorbed by water and marine plants.

Carbon sinks

CO_2 contains a chemical element called **carbon**. Whenever CO_2 is absorbed, the carbon becomes part of whatever absorbed it. Scientists call things that absorb huge amounts of carbon, **carbon sinks**. Soil, forests and oceans are MASSIVE carbon sinks.

There's another set of carbon sinks hidden deep underground. They're known as **fossil fuels**, and they're found in different forms, including...

Crude oil

Natural gas

Coal

Fossil fuels are made of plants and animals that died millions of years ago. They were squashed together when new layers of ground or ocean floor formed on top of them.

How carbon moves around

Usually, carbon moves in a steady cycle from the atmosphere to the ground and back again, often over thousands of years.

Across Earth's history, the amount of carbon in the atmosphere has typically changed very gradually.

CO_2 is in the atmosphere.

Animals and plants respire and give off CO_2.

Plants and oceans absorb CO_2 from the air.

Animals eat plants, which contain carbon.

Droppings and rotting things put carbon into the soil.

As new layers of ground build up, very slowly, fossil fuels form. The carbon is stored here.

What's happening now?

The Earth's temperature has risen very quickly in the past one hundred years, because there's more CO_2 in the atmosphere than there used to be. *More* CO_2 means *more* heat gets trapped. Where is it coming from?

Well, we've been digging up and BURNING lots of fossil fuels, which emits CO_2. And we've REMOVED lots of carbon sinks, for example by cutting down forests. That means less CO_2 is being absorbed.

13

Not just about CO₂

Carbon dioxide has the biggest effect on global heating of all the greenhouse gases. That's because we've emitted SO MUCH of it. But we emit other greenhouse gases that heat the climate, too.

So what *are* the other gases?

Methane (CH₄) which we emit by...

...leaving food to rot in huge piles of waste called landfills.

...turning sewage into clean water.

...extracting fossil fuels from the ground.

...growing rice.

...raising cattle, which burp out CH₄.

...using fertilizers on crops.

Nitrous oxide (N₂O) which comes from...

...burning fossil fuels.

...running air conditioners.

...manufacturing certain chemicals.

Fluorinated gases, or **F-gases**, which we pump out by...

...spraying aerosols and fire extinguishers.

These gases all heat the planet by different amounts. Scientists call the overall impact each one has on global heating its **radiative forcing**.

...making and disposing of refrigerators.

14

The radiative forcing of any gas depends on how LONG it stays in the atmosphere, how MUCH of it there is, and how EFFECTIVE it is at trapping heat.

F-gases
fourth strongest

N_2O
third strongest

CH_4
second strongest

CO_2
strongest radiative forcing

Air pollution

We also emit a lot of other polluting gases. Unlike the main greenhouse gases, which hang around for years, these last just a few days. Scientists think that these gases combined have actually *cooled* our climate. This might sound like a good thing, but they're very bad for our health.

Sulfur and Nitrogen oxides

These come mainly from burning fossil fuels, especially coal, diesel and fuel for ships and planes.

Ozone (O_3)

We don't emit O_3 directly. It forms when other greenhouse gases react in the air.

Black carbon (or soot)

Wildfires, vehicles that run on diesel, and coal power stations all emit black carbon.

The good news is that a lot of these gases come from the SAME human activities that are causing the crisis. So, as we tackle the crisis, we can ALSO improve everyone's health.

Like CO_2, the amount of CH_4, N_2O and F-gases in the atmosphere has increased MASSIVELY in the past century. This is *part* of what's heating the planet.

But it all *started* with CO_2. The crisis would never have gotten so bad if humans hadn't started burning fossil fuels on a large scale...

IPCC

Why fossil fuels are great

When fossil fuels are burned, they release huge amounts of ENERGY. People really first started exploiting that energy about 200 years ago. This completely transformed the world.

Before that, people got most of their energy from working animals and burning wood. Burning wood doesn't produce a lot of energy, and the smoke it gives off is dirty.

It was a mucky time to be alive.

When wood was the main fuel, work was backbreaking, there weren't many jobs and most people lived in poverty.

I have to chop wood twice a day.

About 200 years ago, during a period known as the Industrial Revolution, people discovered that burning fossil fuels was much more powerful than wood. Burning them allowed us to travel further, faster, and make more stuff, more quickly.

Before fossil fuels...	Most things were made by hand. 	People rode around in horse-drawn carts.
Since fossil fuels...	We've been able to power machines to manufacture things for us.	We've powered new vehicles, such as planes and cars.

Exploiting fossil fuels has led to the greatest rise in living standards the world has ever seen.

Especially since 1950, the world's wealth has *exploded*. Some economists call it the GREAT ACCELERATION.

Why fossil fuels *aren't* so great

Whenever we dig up and burn fossil fuels to produce energy, we pump out greenhouse gases. This means extra CO_2 is getting into the atmosphere, and this is making the planet *hotter* by making the greenhouse effect *stronger*.

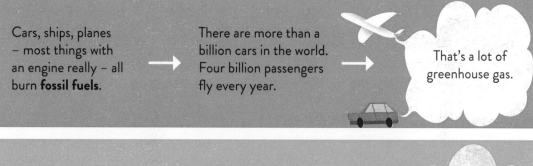

Cars, ships, planes – most things with an engine really – all burn **fossil fuels**.

→ There are more than a billion cars in the world. Four billion passengers fly every year.

→ That's a lot of greenhouse gas.

Lights, computers, smartphones – machines of all kinds – use **electricity**.

→ 66% of electricity comes from power stations that generate power by *burning fossil fuels*.

→ That's *even more* greenhouse gas.

There were about 7.8 billion people alive in 2020 – four times as many as 100 years ago. The more people there are, the more fossil fuels we use. This also means we need more food to eat and more land to live on.

Lots of people eat meat, cheese and yogurt, and drink milk.

→ Farm animals that chew on grass – especially cows and sheep – produce **methane**.

→ There are even more cows than there are cars. That's A LOT of methane.

To fit everything in, we clear forests on a much, MUCH larger scale than when wood was the main fuel.

→ Whenever we remove trees, we STOP them from REMOVING CO_2 from the air.

→ Destroying natural carbon sinks can also RELEASE stored CO_2 back to the air.

Practically EVERYTHING we do is adding extra greenhouse gases to the atmosphere. The heating this causes is having an effect all around the world RIGHT NOW.

So what's happening right now?

Right now, Earth's climate is getting warmer. On average, the world is 1°C hotter than it was 170 years ago (though some places have warmed even more). This change might sound tiny, but it's already had a big effect.

Some natural disasters, such as wildfires, are more severe and last longer.

November 2018

Reporting live from California, USA, where over 18,000 buildings have burned down in the recent fires.

CRISIS!

CRISIS!

The particular place where an animal lives is known as its **habitat**. Climate change and the actions of people are harming many habitats. Some habitats are even disappearing.

If all the trees we nest in die, we'll die too.

CRISIS!

The oceans are absorbing *extra* CO_2. This is making them more acidic.

All sorts of marine life can't handle these conditions.

CRISIS!

Less rain is falling in some places, which means supplies of fresh water are drying up. This is known as a **drought**. It makes it much harder to grow crops and find water to drink.

The rain we rely on didn't come this year.

All over the world, ice that used to be permanent is melting. This is contributing to a rise in sea levels.

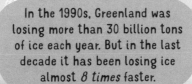

In the 1990s, Greenland was losing more than 30 billion tons of ice each year. But in the last decade it has been losing ice almost *8 times* faster.

CRISIS!

CRISIS!

Some extreme weather events, such as heat waves and floods, are becoming more severe.

Sea levels are 20cm (8 inches) higher than in 1880, and now rising at nearly 4mm (0.15 inches) per year.

The sea around the island we live on is rising. Soon we may not be able to live here anymore.

My town in Bangladesh was washed away.

CRISIS!

How do we know it's getting hotter?

Scientists have calculated world temperatures going back 170 years. Their data shows that the average temperature on Earth varies a little each year. Here's a chart showing a stripe for every one of those 170 years. Blue stripes are colder than the average. Red stripes are warmer. The darker the red, the hotter the year.

1850

Now

You can see that 18 of the 19 warmest years on record have occurred since 2001.

This phenomenon is often called GLOBAL HEATING.

https://showyourstripes.info

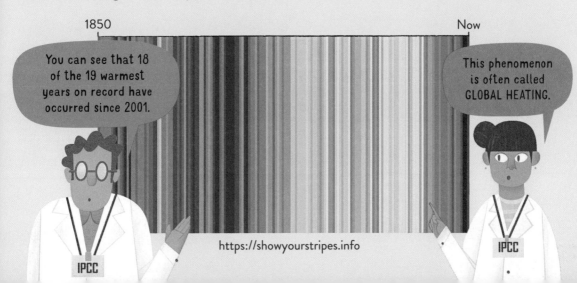

Hotter and hotter

Global heating isn't just about greenhouse gases. Parts of the climate react in ways which make the heating stronger. One example is how much of the Sun's energy gets absorbed, measured as **albedo** – the scientific word for how reflective a surface is.

Albedo is REALLY important. The less energy the Earth reflects, the hotter it gets.

IPCC

Glacier, made of ice

Paler things, such as clouds and ice, have *high* albedo and **REFLECT** a lot of energy. So high albedo ice is vital for keeping us cool. We wouldn't want albedo to be *too* high though – we'd all freeze.

Darker things, such as the sea or forests, have a *low* albedo and **ABSORB** more energy.

Feedback loops

A consequence of global heating is that *more* ice and snow is melting. When they melt, a high albedo surface is replaced with a low one.

...AND SO ON.

This creates *more* warming, which means *more* ice melts, which means *more* low albedo surfaces, creating *more* warming...

When an effect makes it more likely that the same effect will happen again, it's called a **feedback loop**. Not all feedback loops are bad news, but this one is.

Tipping points

Usually the climate changes gradually, or not at all. But sometimes, one small change can cause something called a **tipping point**. And then, dramatic changes happen fast – and you can't easily go back.

It's a little like gently nudging a vase towards the edge of a table.
It's fine...

...until it's not.

SMASH

A tipping point in Earth's climate may have been crossed in the Arctic.

Beneath my feet is ground that remains frozen throughout the year. This is known as PERMAFROST.

Much of the permafrost is made of dead plants that can't rot because they are frozen. But when the ground thaws enough, the dead plants CAN rot. As they rot, they release greenhouse gases.

Past a certain amount, the thawing will be extremely hard to reverse. This is because of ANOTHER feedback loop.

Releasing more greenhouse gases will fuel global heating, and make more of the permafrost thaw...

...releasing more greenhouse gases...

...AND SO ON.

How much will thaw?

Not all of it. But it's still estimated that, by 2100, thawing permafrost could release 30 times as much greenhouse gas as humans emitted in 2020.

Our complicated climate

The climate is **complicated** and **interconnected**.
Just look at this diagram. It shows how increasing the temperature sets off changes to the climate, the weather and the planet.

Start here.

Earth gets hotter

Winds change

The atmosphere moves heat and water around the world with wind and clouds. This controls the weather.

Land warms

Lands warms 1.5 times faster than the planet overall.

Sea warms

Warmer water also expands, causing sea levels to rise.

Sea levels rise

Beaches disappear. Land is washed away. There's more severe flooding during storms, and coastal areas flood more frequently.

Ocean currents change

Ocean currents move heat around the world. Warmer seas change the way currents work. Fresh water from melted ice also has an effect.

KEY:

Heat ➡️

Air ➡️

Water ➡️

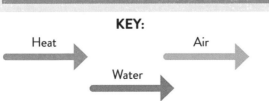

Clouds change

Cloud patterns are very sensitive to changes in the sea and wind. Changes in clouds affect rainfall and Earth's albedo.

Wetter weather in many places

Global heating makes extreme rainstorms more likely. Warmer air holds more water.

More floods

Loss of carbon sinks

Hotter, drier weather in many places

Heat waves become more likely and last longer. Hot, humid weather is particularly deadly.

Wildfires

Fires start more easily and last longer when it's hotter and drier.

Mountain snow and glaciers melt

Glaciers supply water for many rivers. As ice melts, rivers' flows will change. More water will run into the sea.

Water crisis

Less water from rains and rivers mean droughts last longer.

WOW! It really is complicated. But how does this affect *us*?

23

The human cost

How is the crisis likely to affect *you*? The answer depends a lot on where you live. Many people have *already* been affected, especially people in the poorest countries, and over time more and more will be.

Health

In many places, human health will face new threats.

Don't stay out for too long. It's dangerous!

Hmm... I haven't seen this disease in Europe before.

Parts of northern India and other places are predicted to become unbearably hot. Above a certain humidity and temperature, the body can no longer cool itself enough to survive for long.

As the climate changes, the places where you can catch diseases will change too. For example, malaria, which is carried by warm-loving mosquitoes, could spread a lot further, and infect new people.

Jobs and work

Climate change will stop many people from being able to work and earn money.

I can't work here now.

A number of studies predict that the biggest financial cost of climate change will be how it stops people from working, particularly outdoors.

Drought

In places that get hotter and drier, water will be harder to come by.

Without water, we have no crops. Without crops, we have nothing to eat.

rumble

Scientists predict that Central America, the southwest USA, and countries around the Mediterranean Sea will be affected the worst by drought.

Migration and violence

Many people will be forced to move, or **migrate**, to escape dangerous climate conditions.

Fiji, Pacific Ocean

Shortages of living space, food and water can put stress on an already difficult situation. If there aren't good plans to share those things, people might start FIGHTING over them.

Worry

Reading predictions like these can feel overwhelming. The stress and uncertainty affects a lot of people, particularly children.

Caring for the planet means caring for *yourself*, too. This book has lots of ideas about how to approach the crisis healthily, compassionately and proactively. To start with, there are already jobs people are doing that help...

Who will fix it?

When a problem is this big, there's no way that one person can be an expert in every part of it. Any fix will need the help of many different kinds of people. Some are scientists, but there are many more who aren't.

The scientists

But really, EVERYONE is going to have to get involved...

I'm *adapting* my home.

I want to run a green business.

We make decisions that affect whole countries.

Ordinary people

Business owners

Politicians

If I use the right materials and put in shutters...

...then I will stay cool in hot weather.

I'm developing artificial meat so we need fewer cows.

What if we make it more expensive to dig up and burn fossil fuels?

Or give rewards to people who buy non-polluting cars?

What great ideas!

We want to change the way people do things.

What can I do?

WE WANT CHANGE!

CLIMATE JUSTICE!

Activists

YOU!

The first and best thing that anyone – including you – can do is learn about what's going on. The rest of this book contains a lot MORE information about the crisis. You'll learn some things you can try now, and others you can do when you're older.

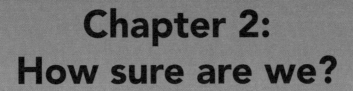

Chapter 2:
How sure are we?

There seem to be so many different opinions about *whether* climate change is happening, how *bad* it is, and what we can actually *do*.

Climate scientists have been working hard to gather the facts. This means we CAN be sure about lots of things, but not *everything*...

Reasonable doubts?

Some people believe that the warnings of climate activists are exaggerated, unnecessary or just wrong. Others believe scientists aren't worried enough.

Aren't we just warming because we're coming out of an ice age?

DAD! HAVEN'T YOU BEEN LISTENING TO ME AT ALL?!

Dad, stop pushing her buttons. And Dani, stop falling for it!

Here are some strong and contradictory opinions about the crisis.

The climate has changed before and recently. This is all part of a NATURAL cycle.

Civilization is going to COLLAPSE by 2030 because of climate change.

The climate is changing because of COSMIC RAYS from outer space. Burning fossil fuels doesn't make any difference.

Computer predictions are completely UNRELIABLE.

If we go past 1.5°C hotter the climate will RUN AWAY with itself.

The SCIENTISTS can't even AGREE about what's going on.

Whenever people publicly express their views, it's important to make sure they can prove or back up what they say. Scientists always question everything – it's a vital part of how science is done.

Do scientists agree?

Because there are so many different views out there, it can give the impression that there is no agreement about the basics of the climate crisis.

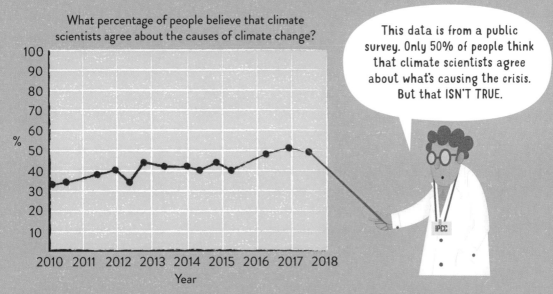

What percentage of people believe that climate scientists agree about the causes of climate change?

%

100
90
80
70
60
50
40
30
20
10

2010 2011 2012 2013 2014 2015 2016 2017 2018
Year

This data is from a public survey. Only 50% of people think that climate scientists agree about what's causing the crisis. But that ISN'T TRUE.

IPCC

In fact, studies of the climate research published in the last decade show that **97%** of all active climate scientists *agree* that global warming is happening and that it is caused by human activity. The **weight of evidence** is overwhelming.

IT'S COSMIC RAYS!!!!

It REALLY isn't.

When the vast majority of scientists agree like this, it's called a **consensus**. The main reason there is now such a strong consensus about climate change is the careful work of the **IPCC**. To find out what that is, turn the page.

The IPCC

IPCC stands for *Intergovernmental Panel on Climate Change*. Set up in the 1980s, it is responsible for giving governments independent scientific advice on the causes of climate change, its impacts and future risks, and how we can reduce those risks.

HI! My name is Nimrita. I am a professor of climate science and I also collaborate with the IPCC.

The IPCC coordinates groups of experts that study ALL climate research that scientists publish around the world. Every 5-7 years the IPCC brings out a report explaining what these experts agree is the latest and best information.

We take *thousands* of pieces of research and boil them down to a single report.

FINAL REPORT 2014

These reports are the most reliable source of information about the climate crisis. The fifth IPCC report came out in 2014. The next one will be published in 2022. In between, they also bring out smaller reports on more specialized topics.

Each report is split into three parts. The first describes what is going on NOW with the climate, and what could happen in the FUTURE.

The second looks at the IMPACTS of climate change on people and the world.

The third part describes what ACTIONS might be taken to stop climate change.

When IPCC scientists check each piece of research, they ask the same awkward questions that you might ask whenever *YOU* check a piece of information. Checking *everything* is a really important part of thinking about science.

Is the author a climate expert? Are they an expert about *this particular topic* as well?

How many experts agree with the author's view?

Is the author clear about how they did their research?

The numbers just don't add up.

Does the author provide references and calculations you can check for yourself?

Is the information up to date?

CLEAN COAL REPORT

Does the author make clear what they *don't know?*

What kinds of predictions does the IPCC make?

Making precise predictions about the future climate is difficult. So much of what will happen depends on what people decide to do over the next few years, and the impact of uncertain tipping points.

How much will the climate warm by 2100?

? ? ? ? ?

0° 0.5° 1° 1.5° 2° 2.5° 3° 3.5° 4° 4.5° 5° 5.5° 6° 6.5° 7°

We don't like to make forecasts that say how likely one particular future is to happen.

Instead we talk about scenarios: "If *this* happens THEN we can expect *this* future." For example...

If we remove all the CO_2 we emit from 2050 onwards, *then* we have a chance of limiting warming to only 1.5°C.

IPCC

How certain is the IPCC?

It's really important to understand that there are parts of climate science that scientists are *less* certain about being *right* about than others. They would never want you to think that they have ALL the answers.

The IPCC uses this scale to show how certain they are in an assessment:

IPCC Certainty	What does that mean?
Virtually certain	99-100% chance of being right
Extremely likely	95-100% chance of being right
Likely	66-100% chance of being right
About as likely as not	33-66% chance of being right

The IPCC thinks it is *likely* that droughts will get worse globally.

The IPCC thinks it is *extremely likely* that human activity has been the main cause of warming since 1950.

Clouds and rainfall are tricky!

I am virtually certain that the Sun will rise tomorrow.

IPCC

Some difference in certainty can be due to the size or **scale** of a question. Scientists are less certain about predicting future climate at small scales (towns and cities) than large global and continental scales.

Some can be due to the **complexity** of a question. Scientists are less confident about predicting complex issues that involve people – such as wars or migration – than simpler climate effects such as heat waves.

You mean you CAN'T tell me *exactly* what's going to happen here in Springfield? Psssh!

I never thought people would help strangers like that.

REFUGEES WELCOME

Some questions to answer...

So if you're so uncertain, that means you might still be *WRONG* about what's going to happen?

I'm sure we are wrong about *some* things – but uncertainty cuts both ways.

Some things might not be as bad as we predict. Others might be much worse. We can't rule out really dire impacts under high warming scenarios, so it's sensible to *act now*.

Is science really all about consensus? Isn't it about discovering NEW things too?

Yes, you're absolutely right. But consensus is REALLY important for anyone trying to make an informed decision – whether it's a government, a business or an individual.

Before you made up your mind, you'd want to know what the experts agreed on, wouldn't you?

I heard that there's a lot of *pressure* on the IPCC to put the best spin on the risks we face.

Every word in an IPCC report has to be okayed by scientists and governments.

Getting everyone to agree involves making COMPROMISES.

That means I don't get to say everything I think, exactly how I want to. But it also means world leaders can't just say what they think people want to hear.

What are IPCC reports used for

Governments and international organizations decide how we deal with the crisis. They use IPCC reports to help them decide what to tackle and how to do it.

After the 2014 IPCC report was released, all the countries in the world met for a huge conference in Paris in 2015.

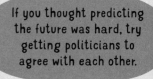

If you thought predicting the future was hard, try getting politicians to agree with each other.

The previous meeting, in 2009, had ended *without* an agreement. So there was enormous pressure on everyone in Paris to compromise. The conference was seen as a final chance. If they failed, collective global efforts could have been finished.

Agreement!

The Paris conference was the biggest ever gathering of world leaders. After two weeks of fierce negotiation, arguments were still raging. Finally – at the last possible moment – an agreement was reached.

THE PARIS AGREEMENT

is a worldwide promise. Almost all countries pledged, for the first time ever, to hold global temperature rise to well below 2°C (above the levels beforewe started burning a lot of fossil fuels). They also said they would *try* to keep the rise to no more than 1.5°C.

Signed

The World

The only way to limit temperature rise to well below 2°C is to rapidly reduce greenhouse gas emissions. In 2018 the IPCC also produced a new report about how quickly emissions needed to be cut to achieve the 1.5°C target.

The 2018 report was extremely ALARMING. But it also had a HOPEFUL message.

IPCC REPORT 2018

- A temperature rise of 1.5°C will cause much less damage than a rise of 2°C.

- To hit this new target, we will need to balance emissions and removals of CO_2 by 2050. This is known as hitting **net zero**.

- **This is achievable** – but it needs a transformation across all of society, *very quickly*.

Researchers have used the information in the report to estimate how much global average temperatures might rise in various scenarios. Although there is uncertainty, it is clear that we must do more if we are going to hit our 1.5°C target.

Global average temperature increase by 2100

How high will it go?

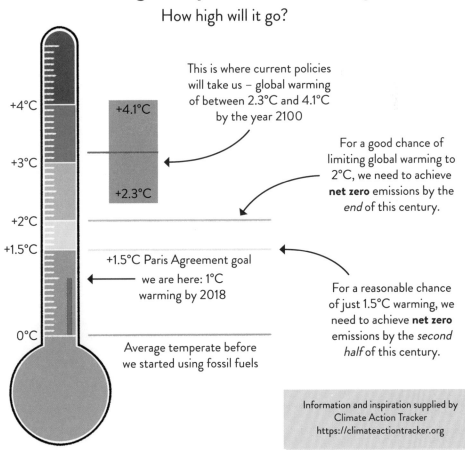

+4°C

+4.1°C

This is where current policies will take us – global warming of between 2.3°C and 4.1°C by the year 2100

+3°C

+2.3°C

For a good chance of limiting global warming to 2°C, we need to achieve **net zero** emissions by the *end* of this century.

+2°C

+1.5°C

+1.5°C Paris Agreement goal
we are here: 1°C warming by 2018

For a reasonable chance of just 1.5°C warming, we need to achieve **net zero** emissions by the *second half* of this century.

0°C

Average temperate before we started using fossil fuels

Information and inspiration supplied by Climate Action Tracker
https://climateactiontracker.org

How do we cut emissions?

First, we have to break down where emissions are coming from. The 5th IPCC report did exactly that. The key lesson is that ALMOST EVERYTHING WE DO emits carbon. Cutting is going to be a challenge.

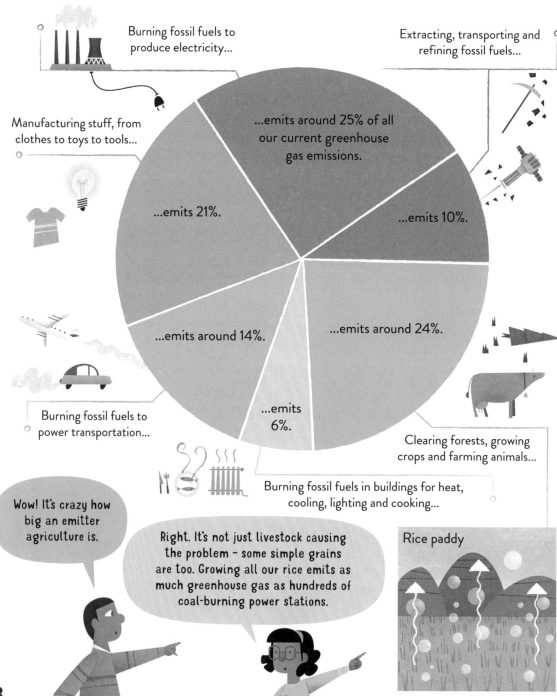

Burning fossil fuels to produce electricity...

Extracting, transporting and refining fossil fuels...

Manufacturing stuff, from clothes to toys to tools...

...emits around 25% of all our current greenhouse gas emissions.

...emits 21%.

...emits 10%.

...emits around 14%.

...emits around 24%.

...emits 6%.

Burning fossil fuels to power transportation...

Clearing forests, growing crops and farming animals...

Burning fossil fuels in buildings for heat, cooling, lighting and cooking...

Wow! It's crazy how big an emitter agriculture is.

Right. It's not just livestock causing the problem – some simple grains are too. Growing all our rice emits as much greenhouse gas as hundreds of coal-burning power stations.

Rice paddy

How much global temperatures rise in the future depends on the total amount of carbon we emit. In 2019, we pumped out 43.1 billion tons of CO_2, the most ever emitted in a single year. To fix the crisis, we have to *shrink* this huge number.

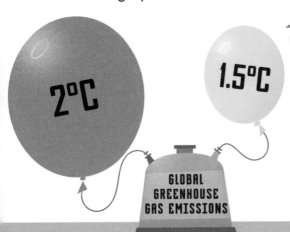

2°C

1.5°C

GLOBAL GREENHOUSE GAS EMISSIONS

Each target – whether 2°C or 1.5°C – has what's called a CARBON BUDGET: a TOP LIMIT to how much we can emit and still keep warming BELOW that temperature.

If we keep emitting as much as we did in 2019, we have 8 years until we use up all the carbon budget for 1.5°C of warming.

POP!

1.5°

To avoid popping the 1.5°C balloon, global CO_2 emissions need to fall 45% by 2030.

This means we need to change the way we do EVERYTHING. It's a mammoth project.

For example, all the power plants, cars and factories that we've already built...

...may emit more than the *entire* carbon budget for 1.5°C of warming over their lifetimes.

That means we can't just stop building NEW fossil fuel burning power plants. We may have to stop using lots of the ones we've ALREADY built.

The difference 0.5°C makes

The difference between 1.5 and 2°C of warming by 2100 may not sound like much, but it will be the difference between life and death for many people, not to mention entire habitats. Here are the IPCC's predictions.

	1.5°C	2°C
Sea ice	In summer, the Arctic free of sea ice once every **100 years**.	In summer, the Arctic free of sea ice once every **10 years**.
Hunger	Fewer fish to catch. Bad harvests more common, especially in dry areas.	Fish catch declines by **twice** as much. Bad harvests are **twice** as likely to happen.
Extreme heat	Percentage of global population exposed to deadly heat waves at least once every five years = **14%**	Percentage of global population exposed to deadly heat waves at least once every five years = **37%**
Species Loss	*Living things losing at least half their habitat include...*	
	6% of insects **8%** of plants **4%** of vertebrates	**18%** of insects **16%** of plants **8%** of vertebrates

Sometimes it's hard to picture what numbers like these mean. So here's just one example of a habitat that's under threat: coral reefs.

70-90% of tropical coral reefs wiped out by 2100.	**99%** of tropical coral reefs are wiped out by 2100.

Right now, it doesn't look likely that we're going to make our warming targets. In fact, the world could warm by more than 3°C and *perhaps* even more than 4°C. This would create the kinds of landscapes you normally see in disaster movies.

Here's how the world *could* look in 2100 with 4°C of warming
(according to Professor Richard Betts, head of Climate Impacts at the Met Office)

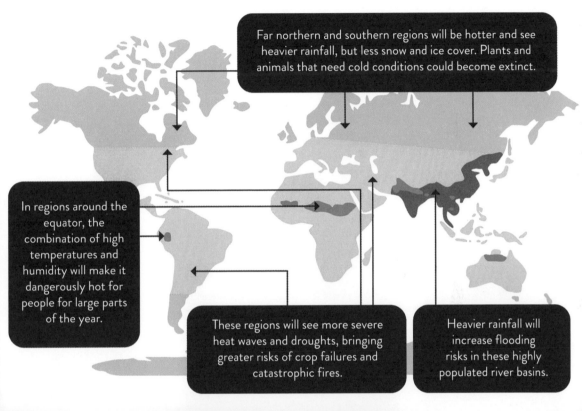

Far northern and southern regions will be hotter and see heavier rainfall, but less snow and ice cover. Plants and animals that need cold conditions could become extinct.

In regions around the equator, the combination of high temperatures and humidity will make it dangerously hot for people for large parts of the year.

These regions will see more severe heat waves and droughts, bringing greater risks of crop failures and catastrophic fires.

Heavier rainfall will increase flooding risks in these highly populated river basins.

OK! OK! I get it. I don't want the world to end up like this.

Great! And thank you. I know how hard it is to change your mind.

But I don't feel better! I don't see how we can do this, and now I'm really WORRIED.

Don't worry, Dad. I'm sure Dani's got a plan...

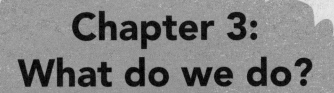

Chapter 3: What do we do?

What does 'solving' the climate crisis actually mean? *Reversing* climate change? *Limiting* how much we emit? Or just carrying on and *adapting*?

We have a CHOICE – in fact, LOTS of choices, for almost everything we do as individuals, businesses and whole societies. Can we make the changes we need to limit heating to 1.5°C?

Are you alright Dad? You look as if you've seen a ghost.

I just had a horrific daydream about the future. We NEED to change things.

Let's find out how...

What makes a good choice?

Whether we're trying to reduce our emissions, or adapt to new conditions, we will have to ask the following questions about whatever we choose to do. Ideally, the answer to each one will be YES.

1. Is it fair?

Some people are worse affected than others by the crisis – particularly poorer people. Our choices need to take this into account. Ideally, the choices we make won't put anybody at a big disadvantage.

> If you ban vehicles in cities, will it still be easy for people with disabilities to get around?

> I'll lose my job on this oil field if we suddenly stop using fossil fuels. That's not fair!

> Our country pollutes less than yours, but WE'RE more at risk from the crisis. YOU should pay to repair the damage!

WORLD POLLUTION SUMMIT

> Build a spaceship that collects energy from the Sun and beams it back to Earth? We don't have the technology!

2. Is it possible?

Even if an idea would work *in theory*, it has to work *in practice* to be useful.

SPACE SOLAR

> And even if we did, it would cost TRILLIONS. That's too much.

We could REWARD companies for emitting less CO_2?

LOW CARBON CASH PRIZE

3. Will people actually do it?

Good solutions are deliberately designed to make sure people are motivated to do them.

People might buy eco-friendly things if they were CHEAPER!

100% HEMP CLOTHING

If we make cutting down forests ILLEGAL, will people stop?

I'd recycle more if it wasn't so confusing.

SAVE THE TREES!!!

STOP FELLING!

PLASTIC FABRIC PAPER GLASS GENERAL WASTE

Messy choices

In reality, most choices will be a bit messy – they'll have a mixture of positive and negative consequences. So we'll have to choose what sacrifices we are willing to make.

They should build a dam here to power our city using water, not fossil fuels.

NO! Dams can harm the plants and animals that live in the river!

But we need to stop using fossil fuels! Which is more important, Dani!?

What are our options?

Basically, governments and people have two broad paths to follow as they try to find solutions to the huge challenges of the climate crisis.

1. Stop the crisis from getting worse

Some solutions try to avoid or limit the impact that climate change will have *before the impact happens*. This is known as **mitigation**. A lot of the solutions in this book are what's called mitigation strategies. Here's an example:

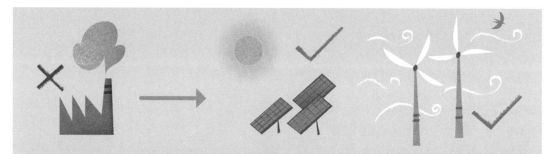

When we generate power without emitting greenhouse gases using sources such as sunlight and wind, it's known as **clean energy**. Replacing coal-burning power stations with clean power generation LOWERS the carbon emissions which cause climate change.

2. Adapt to the impacts of the crisis

Some impacts from the climate crisis have already happened, and others cannot be avoided in the future. So people will have to **adapt** the way they live. That means we will need to prepare or do things *differently*.

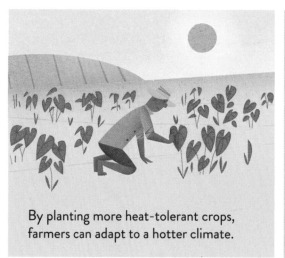

By planting more heat-tolerant crops, farmers can adapt to a hotter climate.

Awnings on all windows for shade

Governments can change the rules so new houses are built differently, to keep cooler in higher heat.

There is also a third option, although it is not one that many would choose: let the crisis unfold, and suffer. In fact, *whatever* we do, there will be some consequences of the climate crisis that we cannot avoid.

The question becomes, how much suffering do we want to put up with?

The more we can MITIGATE, the fewer impacts we'll have to ADAPT to, and so the less anyone will have to suffer.

Well let's get going! Where's the best place to start?

The economy

The system that everyone in the world uses to buy and sell everything – from hot peppers to houses to jobs – is known as the **economy**. Every climate crisis strategy and solution has to take the economy into account...

As economists, Sara and I know that the way our economy works doesn't always help the climate crisis.

But we need solutions NOW, Enofe. We don't have time to come up with a completely new way of running the economy.

Often, businesses and people feel encouraged to make as much PROFIT as possible, even if that harms the climate.

Instead, we have to adjust what the economy does well, to try to reduce the problems that it creates. Let us try to explain...

Small choice, big impact

The world's economy is a vast network of moving money that connects every person, business and government. But though it's big and complicated, it's powered by one small, simple thing: people's choices.

Choices and markets

In the economy, **markets** are where buyers and sellers come together. Every time you (and everyone else) makes a CHOICE – to *buy* or *not to buy* something – you are sending a signal to the market.

> Where should we go for the Summer?

UGANDA

LAOS   BRAZIL

The amount that people want to buy of a product is known as the **demand**.

The amount that businesses can sell of a product is known as the **supply**.

> Oh dear! These cheap flights are popular. I hope we get one.

> I'm sorry. We've just sold the last seat...

CHEAPO AIR
DISCOUNT FLIGHTS

> We need more seats to sell. Buy planes!

If there's **more** demand than there is supply, it sends a signal to sellers to supply **more** product to the market – or to **raise** their prices.

> Oh no! We bought too many planes. Now we can't sell all our seats.

If there's **less** demand than there is supply, it sends a signal to sellers to supply **less** product or **lower** their prices.

Wait a sec! That's very interesting, but how is it relevant to the climate crisis?

Because YOUR choices MATTER. Every one you make sends signals to the market.

When you buy a plane ticket, you are sending an instruction to the market that you want more planes to fly, and more airports to be built.

When you choose not to fly, you are saying the OPPOSITE. Fewer planes, fewer runways, fewer airports and LESS greenhouse gas.

Really? If we don't buy seats on a plane, surely someone else will just buy them instead. The plane will take off with or without us.

This plane might, sure. But the next one might not if more people start making the same decision.

If enough people make a choice, markets will respond. That's how they work.

There's real value in standing up for what you believe in. Studies show that people are more likely to fly *less* if they know someone who has given up flying because of the climate crisis. That's another feedback loop – but this time a good one.

To fight the climate crisis better, we have to make sure that markets are HELPING people, businesses and countries make the right kinds of choices.

Luckily, we've got a few tricks up our sleeve to do just that...

Helping people make better choices

Whether it's the *promise* of a reward, the *threat* of a punishment, or the subtle *nudge* of just the right piece of information, anything that encourages you to make a particular choice is an **incentive**.

Money is a common incentive. For instance, a government could give everyone $100 to buy a new bike. This might encourage people to buy bikes.

When a government pays to make something cheaper, it's known as a **subsidy**. The benefit for the government here is that more bikes = fewer cars = fewer emissions.

Something that discourages you from a particular choice is known as a **disincentive**.

--- TAX BILL ---
MAXX OIL
To pay:
$77,000,000,
000,000,000

A **tax** is money that people and businesses have to pay to the government. Taxing businesses for emitting greenhouse gases might discourage them from polluting.

The wrong kind of subsidies

Incentives can also be unhelpful if they're applied to the wrong thing. Instead of discouraging people from using fossil fuels, a 2016 survey found that 112 nations *subsidized* fossil fuels, usually to make energy more affordable for their citizens.

In 2017 governments spent $370 billion subsidizing fossil fuels compared with $110 billion for clean energy.

Switching those subsidies around, would go a long way to starting a clean energy revolution.

The true cost

Markets are meant to help buyers and sellers find the right price. But sometimes markets fail because they don't take everything into account.

A factory produces a lot of cheap teddy bears. But part of its production process releases a lot of greenhouse gases into the atmosphere.

Cleaning up that mess is expensive. But Mega Bear doesn't pay for it. Other people will have to pay to clean up the pollution later on. The bears are cheap and popular.

The only way to fix this is for the government to pass laws that make businesses pay for the TRUE COST of their pollution. Now, for the business to make a profit, it will need to charge much more for its teddy bears.

This high cost incentivizes the business to find ways of producing teddy bears that DON'T produce so much greenhouse gas. This way it won't have to pay for the clean up and its costs will be lower.

How much *is* the true cost?

When governments make people and businesses pay to emit carbon, it is known as a **carbon price**. Many politicians and economists believe that this is a good idea – the tricky part is agreeing what the price should be.

The main point is that the price should be HIGH enough to INCENTIVIZE everyone to change their habits. This may be unpopular with businesses that rely on making money from fossil fuels.

This is going to cost me a lot of money!

Fuel is too expensive! We can't do our jobs.

Another concern is that spending more money is easier if you are rich, so higher prices will *unfairly* disadvantage poorer people. In recent years, workers whose jobs were affected have protested against carbon prices.

Others point out that a carbon price works best when every country agrees to it. If some people and businesses don't pay for their pollution, they will have an unfair advantage.

VS.

ECO BEAR
$7

MEGA BEAR
$5

15%
A recent study found that only 15% of all of the world's emissions are covered by a carbon price.

¾ < $10
The same study found that three quarters of all carbon prices are $10 or less per ton of carbon.

The IPCC has shown that for a good chance of achieving our 1.5°C goal, by 2030 the carbon price for ALL EMISSIONS needs to be $100-200 per ton of CO_2 emitted.

That's much higher than most carbon prices are now. So getting everyone to agree is going to be a HUGE challenge.

Investing

For governments, one benefit of getting money from a carbon tax is that it can be used to increase spending on things that *help* the climate crisis. Spending money on projects or businesses is known as **investing**.

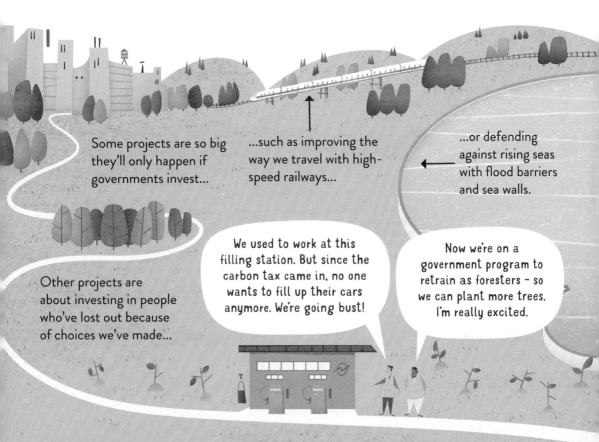

Some projects are so big they'll only happen if governments invest...

...such as improving the way we travel with high-speed railways...

...or defending against rising seas with flood barriers and sea walls.

Other projects are about investing in people who've lost out because of choices we've made...

We used to work at this filling station. But since the carbon tax came in, no one wants to fill up their cars anymore. We're going bust!

Now we're on a government program to retrain as foresters - so we can plant more trees. I'm really excited.

A government's investments show what they care about. That's true for businesses and people too. Some have started *only* investing in companies that take climate change seriously. The more people do this, the more pressure the market will put on ALL companies to care about their environmental impact.

So what projects should the government run? Do you have any ideas?

So many. It's hard to know where to start!

Burning less fossil fuel sounds like a good place to start...

What do we do about energy?

Energy use currently contributes about two thirds of all global emissions. If we want to meet the global target of no more than 1.5°C of warming by 2100, we will have to make BIG CHANGES to how we supply and use energy.

We have to leave fossil fuels in the ground. Burning them all just emits too much greenhouse gas.

But DEMAND for energy keeps growing! So the trillion dollar question is how do we get everyone the energy they need?

For its 2018 report, the IPCC looked at many different solutions to this problem. The plans all had different approaches, but some common strategies emerged.

1. We should **switch** our electricity supply away from dirty fossil fuels. Instead, we have to supply as much electricity as possible from **clean sources** that emit fewer greenhouse gases than burning fossil fuels.

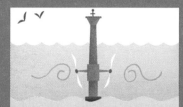

Tidal power uses the movement of tides to generate power.

Solar power gets energy from the Sun.

Water from rivers and dams is used to generate hydroelectric power.

Guess where wind power gets it energy from?

Energy supplied by nuclear power does not emit greenhouse gases.

Burning plants can produce energy. With carbon capture (see p. 58) it can remove CO_2 too.

54

2. We should use less energy per person. The lower our **demand** for energy, the easier it will be to meet our target.

A low demand lets us pick and choose how we supply clean energy.

We could pick THESE options...

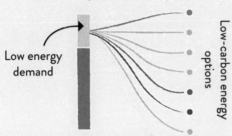

Low energy demand

Low-carbon energy options

...or we could pick THOSE options.

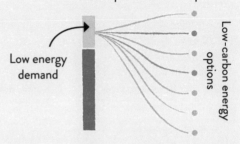

Low energy demand

Low-carbon energy options

A high demand for energy means we'll have NO choice but to use *every* available option if we want to hit our target – and some options are much more expensive or difficult, or both.

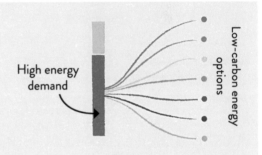

High energy demand

Low-carbon energy options

There are lots of ideas in the rest of this book about how we can use less energy.

3. We should **stop burning dirty fuels** to heat homes, cook meals and power vehicles. Instead, we should switch to using fuels such as clean electricity or cleanly-produced hydrogen, which forms water when it burns.

In many places, a lot of strong greenhouse gases, such as methane and black carbon, are released by people cooking over fires that burn charcoal, dung or wood. Providing everyone with clean electric cooking stoves would improve air quality and reduce greenhouse gas emissions.

Moving beyond fossil fuels

Of the many challenges we face for lowering emissions, changing how we supply and use energy is perhaps the biggest. As you might imagine, it also generates a lot of debate.

There's simply no way that solar power is going to work here in the UK. Have you seen our weather?

That's not true! Solar power DOES work in countries which aren't so sunny. And when it's super sunny, it's amazing. If we could fill a 228 square mile patch of the Sahara Desert with modern solar panels, they would meet ALL the world's energy needs.

That's just 0.1% of the total land surface of the Earth!

But that would never work! How would you get energy from the Sahara to Australia?

You're right – that particular idea isn't very practical. Better to place solar panels ALL AROUND the world with an improved network of cables to transmit the energy where it's wanted.

But what happens when it's dark?

Well, we're working on lots of ways to store energy to make sure we've got it when we need it.

Don't get me wrong. I like your enthusiasm, but I don't see how it's going to work here.

We have no choice but to try – what would you have as an alternative?

Energy storage solutions:

- very big batteries

- converting solar energy into storable fuels, such as hydrogen

- using solar energy to pump water uphill to generate hydroelectric power later

Cutting energy emissions across the board will be difficult but it is CRUCIAL if we are to hit net zero emissions by 2050. The hope is that changes that seem difficult from one day to the next, might look a bit easier over decades.

Carbon capture

Carbon sinks such as forests and soil are nature's way of absorbing CO_2 from the air. Now humans are inventing their own *artificial* carbon sinks. This is the world of **carbon capture**.

I've caught some!

Ha, good try, but that's not *quite* how it works... most carbon capture involves pumping CO_2 underground and trapping it there for thousands of years.

We can use carbon capture in two key ways:

1. To trap CO_2 *before* it's emitted

In **fossil fuel power plants**, we can separate CO_2 from the fumes in the chimneys...

...pump it through a machine that turns it into liquid...

...then funnel it deep underground, where it's trapped under layers of rock and soil.

If a power plant or factory captures all of the CO_2 it produces, then its emissions fall to ZERO. This is known as being **carbon neutral**.

2. To remove CO₂ *after* it's emitted

If we grow crops to absorb CO_2 from the air, then burn them in a power plant to make electricity, heat or fuel...

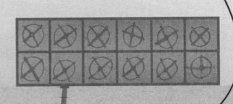

...we can *recapture* the CO_2 and funnel it underground – in the same way we capture it in a carbon neutral fossil fuel power plant. This is known as **BECCS** (Bioenergy with carbon capture and storage).

DACCS (Direct air carbon capture and storage) is another approach. It means sucking in air with huge suction fans, mixing it with chemicals to separate the CO_2...

...then pumping it underground.

BECCS and DACCS are even better than carbon neutral – they're **carbon negative**. That means they remove *more* CO_2 from the air than they emit.

Making it work

If we stop burning fossil fuels we can mitigate the climate crisis. But, to keep warming below 1.5°C, we may well need to suck CO_2 out of the air as well. Carbon capture could be the answer, *if...*

...we can make sure the underground stores won't leak!

...we agree who will pay for it. You can't just expect my oil business to spend money on it for no money in return.

...it doesn't cause more problems than it solves. If we're not careful, BECCS might take up so much cropland and water that we won't be able to grow enough food.

PSHH

Creating carbon sinks

Nature's carbon sinks could help us through the crisis, too.
If we protect or create more of them, we can remove more CO_2
from the air. But currently, we're *losing* carbon sinks...

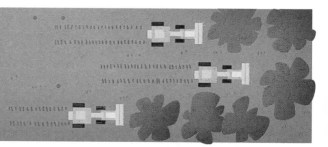

Take tropical rainforests –
studies suggest that we're cutting
and burning down trees *so quickly*
that the forests could soon emit
more CO_2 than they absorb.
What can we do?

The IPCC recommends that we reduce deforestation AND make space to
replant trees where there used to be forest. This is called **reforestation**, and we
know it can work...

South Korea

In the first half of the 20th century, huge
forests in what is now South Korea were
chopped or burned down.

By 1967, vast areas of what was once
lush greenery had become barren.

Barren land is bad news. Trees bring carbon
and water into the soil. Without them, the
ground dries up and little else can grow.

SO, the government
hatched a plan to grow
the forest ALL BACK.

1987

Twenty years later, a
forest 15 times bigger than
London had regrown.

Trees as far as
the eye can see!

The government had incentivized energy
companies to chop down fewer trees to use
as fuel. They'd convinced local landowners
to let them grow trees on their land, too.

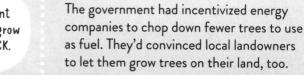

2000

The forests continued to flourish. The larger they grew, the more carbon they stored.

By the late 1990s, they were absorbing and storing **12 TIMES** more carbon every year than before the project began.

According to scientists, a global reforestation project could absorb between 60-200 billion tons of CO_2 this century. That could remove up to a quarter of the CO_2 currently in the air, if it went as well as it possibly could.

Now and beyond

In addition to planting more trees...

Should we chop some of the trees down again?

What? Why?

Young trees absorb carbon more quickly than old trees.

As long as you don't BURN the trees you cut down, they will be a carbon store.

If we then REPLACE the old trees with new ones, *more* CO_2 can then be absorbed. And if we're careful which trees we cut down, it won't harm the wildlife.

Save our soils

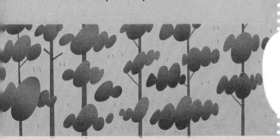

Thick, soggy bogs called **peatlands** store TWICE as much carbon as all the world's forests combined. But we're losing *them*, too. How?

We DRAIN them and BURN them to make land dry enough to farm on. When we do this, the stored carbon goes into the atmosphere.

Really, FARMS are the biggest reason why we're losing carbon sinks. But all that could change...

Smarter farming, smarter eating

What is now farmland used to be wilderness, full of big, natural carbon sinks. If we change how we farm, we can emit less greenhouse gas, use up less space and restore those lost carbon sinks.

Farmers today face a very tough challenge:

People in the world who need feeding	↑ Going up
Greenhouse gases we can emit	↓ Going down
Land we can use	↓ Getting smaller

Um. That doesn't sound easy.

There *are* things we can do though.

The world's food **markets** (see page 48) are going to have to change. This will mean transforming not only how we *farm* (the **supply** side), but also our attitudes to the food that we *buy* (the **demand** side).

Changing our diets

Some foods emit more greenhouse gases and take up more space than others. Meat (especially beef) is the food with the single greatest impact on the climate.

Raising farm animals, or **livestock**, pumps out around 15% of all our emissions.

Worldwide, an area of land twice the size of Russia is used for raising livestock, and growing crops to feed them.

One study calculated that just **halving** how much meat, dairy and eggs people eat in Europe would reduce greenhouse gas emissions in that region by up to **40%**. It would also free up almost a **quarter** of the space that livestock and dairy farms take up. Other studies show similar numbers for the rest of the world, too.

But changing what the world eats is a HUGE task. Solutions will have to take into account the wants and needs of SO many different people...

...on the *supply* side.

I'm a beef farmer. If people eat less meat, how will I make money?

Businesses that make money from selling meat will lose out. How can this be managed fairly?

Financial rewards for farming less meat?

Free training on how to farm *different* foods?

...and on the *demand* side.

We need to stay healthy!

But I LIKE meat!

And I don't know how to cook nice veggie meals...

Meat is a source of **protein** – a nutrient that helps you to grow. If people ate less meat, they would still need protein from somewhere. They could get it from...

If there's a high demand for meat, the supply from farms will stay high too. What might make people buy less?

...nuts.

...peas.

...lentils and beans.

A 'meat tax' to raise the price?

Tasty, affordable meat alternatives?

Better education on cooking with vegetables?

Eating too much meat isn't the only problem. Farming certain types of fruit and vegetables emits a lot too, especially if we transport them far around the world. We'll have to change not just *what* we grow, but *how* and *where* we grow it...

Changing how we grow things

It's impossible to farm food without emitting *some* greenhouse gases – especially from machines. But some farming methods emit more than others, and will have to change.

Nurturing the soil

Farms can reduce emissions by protecting their **soil**. The soil is a huge carbon sink, and the more carbon it has in it, the better it is for growing food.

In crop fields, the soil gets most of its carbon when the crops absorb CO_2 from the air, and pass carbon into the soil through their roots. But there's a problem.

Because of *how* we farm, soil on many farms is losing carbon more quickly than the crops can add it back in.

I churn, or TILL, my fields after every harvest.

Nooo stop! Too much tilling moves carbon from the soil back into the air.

You could plant crops that require less tilling than the ones you grow now.

But that wouldn't work on every farm. A solution's success depends on the climate, crop and soil type. So each farm will need *tailor-made* solutions. Exactly *which* changes happen and work will depend on lots of things.

Will the farm still produce enough to feed everyone who needs it?

Are the right technologies cheap and available?

Will consumers still buy my corn if it looks different?

Some changes are small

Now

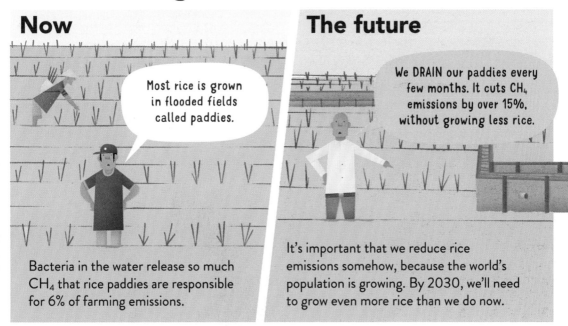

Most rice is grown in flooded fields called paddies.

Bacteria in the water release so much CH_4 that rice paddies are responsible for 6% of farming emissions.

The future

We DRAIN our paddies every few months. It cuts CH_4 emissions by over 15%, without growing less rice.

It's important that we reduce rice emissions somehow, because the world's population is growing. By 2030, we'll need to grow even more rice than we do now.

Some changes are radical

Now

Greenhouse gases from raising livestock are emitted in a number of ways.

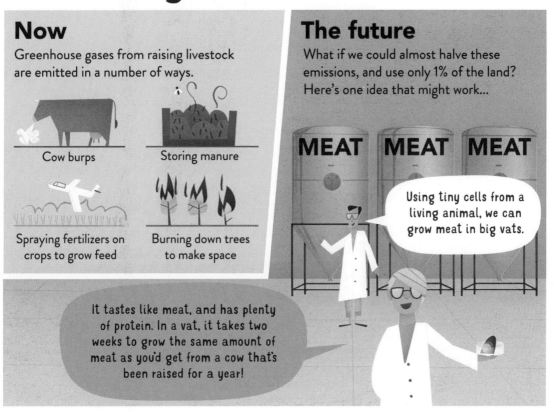

Cow burps

Storing manure

Spraying fertilizers on crops to grow feed

Burning down trees to make space

The future

What if we could almost halve these emissions, and use only 1% of the land? Here's one idea that might work...

MEAT MEAT MEAT

Using tiny cells from a living animal, we can grow meat in big vats.

It tastes like meat, and has plenty of protein. In a vat, it takes two weeks to grow the same amount of meat as you'd get from a cow that's been raised for a year!

Waste not, warm not

A THIRD of the food we produce worldwide gets **wasted**.
This contributes to greenhouse gas emissions in lots of different ways.
Together, they add up to 8-10% of our global emissions.

Food is wasted at every stage of its journey from farm to plate.
Take avocados, for example...

On the farm
Food is wasted when...

...a crop grows badly, so isn't harvested.

...it goes bad while in storage.

...farmers miss bits while harvesting.

...the farmer can't sell all the fruit she has harvested.

On the road
Food is packaged up, then transported by air, sea or road.
It gets wasted when...

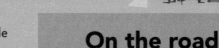

...the packaging breaks and the food goes bad.

...the food gets bruised or damaged by bumping into each other.

...the journey is too long and the food goes bad.

With the buyer
Once the food ends up in supermarkets, restaurants and people's homes, it can go to waste when...

...supermarkets can't sell everything before the sell-by date.

...people throw out leftovers.

Hold on. Waste never sounds like a good thing. But how is all this actually creating emissions?

...people don't use what they buy.

...restaurants buy too much, or cook too much.

Greenhouse gas emissions from food waste happen in a number of ways.

In the landfill

A lot of the food that gets wasted along the journey is left to rot away in a landfill. Food in landfills emits CO_2 and CH_4 as it rots.

Unnecessary fuel and space

If we wasted less food, we'd have a better idea of how much we actually need. It would take less energy to grow, transport and store food if we made less of it in the first place.

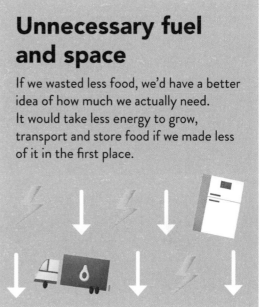

Fixing waste

To solve our waste problem, we won't need bold new ideas. We already have the ideas – we just need to do more of them. Here are a few examples.

On the farm

Many farms harvest with machines, which collect *most* of the crop, but always miss some of it. There are companies that send in people to scavenge harvested crops for anything left over.

On the road

If supermarkets stock food grown LOCALLY, the food wouldn't have to travel as far. This only makes a difference if the food is also grown in a way that doesn't harm the planet.

With the buyer

Many leftovers can be turned into **compost** – a soil-like mulch that helps other plants to grow. Letting food decay this way produces less CH_4 than in a landfill.

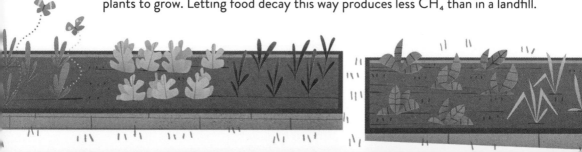

Moving people around

The more people there are, and the richer they get, the more they want to travel. Vehicle emissions make up about 14% of our total greenhouse gas emissions, but they're increasing FASTER than any other type.

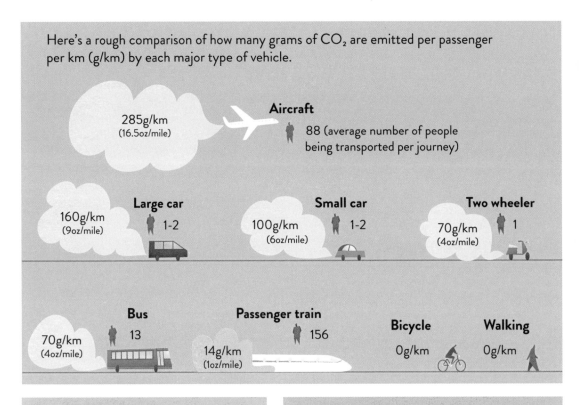

Here's a rough comparison of how many grams of CO_2 are emitted per passenger per km (g/km) by each major type of vehicle.

Aircraft

285g/km
(16.5oz/mile)

88 (average number of people being transported per journey)

Large car

160g/km
(9oz/mile)

1-2

Small car

100g/km
(6oz/mile)

1-2

Two wheeler

70g/km
(4oz/mile)

1

Bus

70g/km
(4oz/mile)

13

Passenger train

14g/km
(1oz/mile)

156

Bicycle

0g/km

Walking

0g/km

Some people travel a lot, while most people hardly travel at all. 10% of all the people in the world account for 80% of all vehicle emissions.

This means there's lots of room for vehicle emissions to grow even further. If the number of flights keeps going up, planes could consume *a quarter* of the world's ENTIRE carbon budget for 1.5°C of warming by 2050.

I've never been on a plane.

#globetrotter

Most journeys are short and local. That's why – *right now* – road emissions from engines in cars and trucks make up about three quarters of vehicle emissions.

Below, is an achievable BLUEPRINT that people, businesses and governments can follow to *reduce* road emissions.

These choices will work best if they all work TOGETHER. It won't do much good to encourage people not to use cars if there are no buses or trains to REPLACE them. We need JOINED-UP solutions.

Avoid journeys where possible

- Towns and cities can be designed more densely so walking is easier than driving.
- Businesses can encourage their workers to work from home.

Provide greener alternatives

- Governments can spend more on trains and buses, to make them cheaper, more efficient and more attractive to use.
- Governments can design roads to make it easier and safer to cycle.

Don't use fossil fuels

- Substitute oil-based fuels for greener fuels such as methane or biofuels.
- Use electric vehicles, although this works best when the electricity is generated by clean sources, rather than burning fossil fuels.

Be more efficient

- Engineers can design lighter cars and improve engines so they use less fuel.
- People can choose to share rides rather than drive alone.
- Encourage new technologies, such as electric bikes.

High-speed trains that zoom between walkable towns and cities make an ATTRACTIVE future.

But we need to deal with FLYING too. At the moment we don't have practical ways to make flights carbon-free.

Follow the footprints

As things are made, moved, used and disposed of, greenhouse gases are released. The amount emitted by each item is known as its **carbon footprint**. It's hard to calculate precisely, but we *can* make reasonable estimates.

Carbon footprints are made up of two parts.

Direct emissions are directly related to the product itself.

Manufacturing the product

Using the product

Shipping the product

Indirect emissions are not caused by the product, but by processes that go on around it.

Emissions caused by producing the materials to make it

Emissions caused by disposing of the product

Emissions caused by people driving to buy the product

British researcher Mike Berners-Lee wrote a book called *How Bad are Bananas?*, estimating the footprints of many different things. He calculated them by estimating the weight in grams (g) of carbon that a product directly, or indirectly, emits. 1g of carbon is around 0.04 ounces – a tiny amount.

A banana's footprint is pretty low. Bananas keep well, so they can be shipped rather than flown. They even come with their own packaging – the peel.

In 2010, the world drank *hundreds of billions* of bottles of water. That's many *millions* of tons of greenhouse gases which could easily be cut back, especially in places with clean drinking water.

10g

80g

145g

160g

500g

A paper towel

A banana

A disposable nappy (or diaper)

A 500 ml (16oz) bottle of water

An ice cream

Cutting footprints

Businesses can look at every stage of how something is made and used to try to cut emissions.

But *people* have carbon footprints too. This isn't just to do with the things they buy, but also to do with the way they live.

The yearly carbon footprint of the average person is 7.5 US tons. But this rises to 30 US tons for the average North American. For tips on how to cut your personal carbon footprint, see page 106.

Cement accounts for about 4% of the world's total greenhouse gas emissions.

A large bag of rice causes more emissions than burning half a gallon of diesel fuel.

A desktop computer takes 30g of carbon / hour to run.

One London to Hong Kong flight has the footprint of around 60,000 bananas.

This final column of the graph would stretch off the page for several miles.

Data hubs are places that keep computers and the internet working. They consume 3% of the world's electricity. That's more than most countries.

Every email you send, video that you watch or picture that you store has a carbon footprint.

910g (32oz)

4kg (9lb)

11.5kg (25lb)

800kg (0.8 US tons)

4.6 tonnes (5.2 US tons)

700 million tonnes (780 million US tons)

1 kg (35oz) of cement

1 kg (35oz) of rice

A pair of shoes

Building a desktop computer

A flight from London to Hong Kong

The world's data hubs combined

Bright lights, green city

By 2050, experts predict that 70% of the world's population will live in busy, bustling cities. To limit global temperature rise to 1.5°C, cities will have to emit much less and absorb much more.

So, what should future cities do differently?

Emitting less

Big changes to how cities are organized and powered can massively cut emissions.

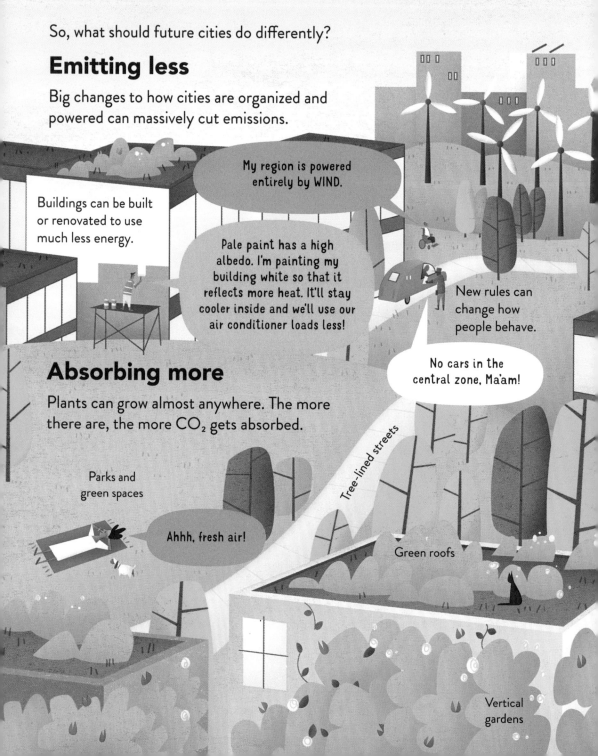

Buildings can be built or renovated to use much less energy.

My region is powered entirely by WIND.

Pale paint has a high albedo. I'm painting my building white so that it reflects more heat. It'll stay cooler inside and we'll use our air conditioner loads less!

New rules can change how people behave.

Absorbing more

Plants can grow almost anywhere. The more there are, the more CO_2 gets absorbed.

No cars in the central zone, Ma'am!

Parks and green spaces

Tree-lined streets

Ahhh, fresh air!

Green roofs

Vertical gardens

Adapting

As well as *mitigating* the effects of the crisis, many cities will have to *adapt* to new living conditions. Exactly *how* cities adapt will differ from place to place, depending on how their local climates change.

The way a city is built may have to be reorganized.

The way people go about their day-to-day lives may have to change.

From a giant flood wall in Rotterdam, Netherlands, that's controlled by a supercomputer, to rules in New Delhi, India, that mean people can only use their car every other day – cities, towns and villages all around the world are already beginning to adapt. Have you noticed adaptations where you live?

Keeping cool

One of the biggest contradictions of global heating is that many of the ways we keep things COOL – be it ice cream, or our homes – actually make the climate HOTTER.

Refrigerants

We put gases called **refrigerants** in air conditioners, refrigerators, freezers and other appliances that keep things cool. They're useful, but dangerous if they end up in the atmosphere.

The most widely used refrigerants are **hydrofluorocarbons**, or **HFCs**. They're really strong greenhouse gases.

In fact, HFCs are MANY THOUSANDS of times stronger than CO_2, so if we emit even slightly too many, global heating will get much worse.

HFC emissions come from...

...manufacturing the appliances that contain them.

...disposing of the appliances.

...leaks.

Currently, HFCs and other refrigerants make up less than 1% of our greenhouse gas emissions. But they're still a big threat, for two reasons.

1. Demand for refrigeration will rise as the world's population goes up and the planet gets hotter, so emissions may rise too.

2. 90% of HFC emissions happen through leaks during disposal. There are *millions* of appliances out there, some decades old, that will need to be disposed of eventually.

Even though HFCs make up such a tiny proportion of our emissions, cutting them out and disposing of them safely could reduce future heating by 0.5°C. By our climate's standards, that's LOADS.

Such a large threat needs a global response. In 2016, officials from over 170 countries met in Kigali, Rwanda, to finalize a plan to stop using HFCs completely.

The Kigali Deal is a good example of a solution that had to be FAIR to work at all.

The deal they reached was a COMPROMISE that everybody was happy with.

The Kigali Deal

- Countries will cut their HFC use by more than three quarters by 2036 and 2047, depending on how wealthy they are.

- Richer countries will give poorer countries money to help them make the change.

- There will be financial punishments for any countries that fail to stick to the plan.

SIGNED:

EXTREME solutions

Changing the ocean, the weather or the ground beneath our feet sound like the kind of schemes a super-villain would come up with – but some scientists have suggested they could help SAVE our planet.

There's a surprising amount we can do with rocks. **Powdered rocks** can absorb a lot of CO_2 – especially if they are spread out thinly on the ground.

I'm going to crush this mountain into gravel!

MEGA CRUSH

The right rocks in the right places could actually help crops GROW BETTER as well.

BUT crushing the rocks into small pieces uses energy, and chemicals that run off the rocks could harm the environment.

Another option might be to use powdered rocks to make the ocean less acidic. This means it will absorb more CO_2.

Alternatively, we could **fertilize the ocean** with iron or nitrogen to encourage algae to grow. Large blooms of algae can suck up and store a lot of CO_2.

Powdered rocks

Algae bloom

Fiddling with ocean systems will be a big risk. Unless we keep doing them forever, these interventions will only keep the CO_2 out of the atmosphere for a short time. If we stop, the CO_2 will be re-released and temperatures will rise again.

There are some *really* BIG ideas for what we could do if we're desperate. These tend to be about directly cooling down the planet by making the Earth's *albedo* higher, so that it reflects more heat.

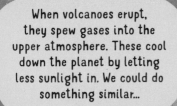

When volcanoes erupt, they spew gases into the upper atmosphere. These cool down the planet by letting less sunlight in. We could do something similar...

Planes could inject the sun-dimming gases really high up. Is it crazy or am I a GENIUS?

We could spray salt into clouds to make them more reflective.

We could cover glaciers with reflective sheets to cool them down.

The problem is, we still don't know how effective these solutions would be – or if they would have unwanted consequences.

What if changing the clouds in one place drastically affected the rainfall somewhere else?

Imagine if every country starts fiddling with the weather! How are people going to keep control of that?

A lot of research remains to be done.

Getting the job done

To limit warming to 1.5°C, our society needs to be carbon neutral by 2050. We'll have to change how we power things, grow food, move around and more – and it'll need to happen FAST. How can we make it happen?

It's a HUGE challenge, but we won't need amazing superpowers to overcome it. In fact, all we'll really need is regular, everyday, human powers – skills that anyone can use...

My power is setting CLEAR GOALS. Whether it's an international treaty, or a plan to adapt your home, every project needs a target to work towards.

Plant 1 million trees!

Captain Target

My power is COMMUNICATION. National and local governments need to keep each other in the loop and share what they know.

LADY LOOP

Be TRUSTWORTHY, like me. Governments need to promise to cut their emissions, and they need to stick to their word.

I possess the power of EXPERTISE. All solutions need to take the latest knowledge into account.

The Professor

REX RELIABLE

GRETA MOVE-ON

ZOOOOM

ZOOOOM

Those skills are all useless without my power – SPEED. No country's current targets will be enough to limit warming to 1.5°C. Let's go, go, GO!

All those skills are essential to create treaties, plans and actions that WORK. According to the IPCC, change is particularly crucial in three areas – technology, money and how we behave – to stand a chance of meeting the 1.5°C target.

Technology

We need to make it possible for technology to advance quickly enough. It also has to be cheap and available everywhere it's needed.

> Give farmers money to spend on climate-friendly machinery. Quick!

ZOOOOM

OOOOM

Money

We need to invest much, much more in technologies, ideas and programs that keep emissions low.

> According to my calculations, we need to invest $20 billion in new wind farms...

> And let's aim to train up 15,000 people to work on them.

How we behave

Governments only have so much power over how people behave. We need to work out how to get people to change their lifestyles *willingly*.

> I've heard people are more likely to be kind to the planet if they talk about it with their friends.

> Putting a symbol on a food product to show that it comes from a low-carbon farm might make people trust it's from a good source.

There are many things we *need* to do, and even more ways we could *choose* to do them. The thing to keep in mind, is that it CAN be done. But will it?

Chapter 4: What's stopping us?

The world has all the knowledge and technology it needs to start tackling the climate crisis – but it isn't happening fast enough. How come?

The problem with problems

Even if you can think of ways to solve a problem, that doesn't mean it'll be easy to put a solution into practice.

Take this problem: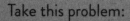

> Argh, one of the wheels came off my skateboard. I need to screw it back on.

As far as problems go, it's not the worst. But Dani is struggling to solve it.

> I don't have the right kind of screwdriver.

> I don't have money to buy one for myself.

> I don't even know *how* to do this.

> I want Ben to help, but he's at a friend's house.

> So many problems. Gah, I give up.

> Your ATTITUDE is the main problem, Dani. Fix that, and you can fix the rest!

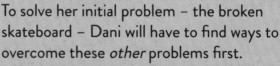

To solve her initial problem – the broken skateboard – Dani will have to find ways to overcome these *other* problems first.

For example, she might ask a friend if they have the correct screwdriver. Or she could ask her parents to lend her money to get the skateboard repaired at a shop.

The climate crisis is a dense knot of problems. There are many different ways to unpick it, but it's proving difficult because – much like with Dani's skateboard – *other* problems are getting in the way.

The population is growing. We need to provide enough energy for all these people to have a good life.

Climate change might be important, but there's a global pandemic – let's deal with *that* first!

This chapter explores a few of these 'other' problems. Some, we'll have to solve. Others, we'll have to live with and work around.

People have different ideas about what the 'other' problems actually *are*, and which ones are more important.

The REAL problem is that lots of rich, polluting companies are just out to get money and don't care about the planet.

No! Those companies give people jobs. The REAL problem is that governments aren't setting the right rules. They should make laws that force businesses to think about the environment.

No, no, NO! PEOPLE are the REAL problem. We all want the good stuff that comes from fossil fuels, so businesses and governments give them to us.

These three people are neither right nor wrong; they just have different opinions. But one thing's for sure – if we're going to stand a chance of dealing with the crisis, we'll have to find ways to work with people we don't agree with.

Who emits and who suffers

Many of the people hit hardest by climate change are poor and vulnerable. They're often the least responsible for the crisis. And even though they're the worst affected, they rarely get a say in big decisions.

Young people

In the future, the children and young people of today will have to deal with the challenging consequences of what older people do NOW.

Most grown-ups only worry about the next few years. They don't care about 50 years in the future, when we'll be in charge.

Women

In many parts of the world, women don't have the same rights as men. They are often paid less, and given fewer opportunities. This makes it harder for them to deal with tough conditions and natural disasters, especially if they have children to look after too.

I wanted to become a doctor, but I had to leave school when I was 13. Now with no job, feeding my family is a daily struggle – ESPECIALLY when a heat wave strikes and dries up our garden soil.

Poor communities

In the world's poorest places, roads, buildings and necessities such as water pipes are sometimes fragile. This puts them at high risk of damage in heatwaves, droughts and floods. And if new illnesses spread to countries that can't afford the best care and protection, it could be disastrous. Here's a made up example...

Mosquitos have brought a new disease to Moldova. The hospitals are already full. They can't afford to treat everybody!

Making it fairer

The idea that climate change is unfair but should be *made* fair, is known as **climate justice**. People have lots of ideas about how it could happen.

Include everyone

One way to include many views is to invite people of different ages and backgrounds to discuss an important issue. The group then recommends to the government what they think should happen. These groups are sometimes known as **citizens' assemblies.**

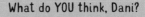

What do YOU think, Dani?

Educate

Changing the rules to make sure girls can stay in school for longer, for example, gives them more skills and opportunities for work when they're older.

I'm a doctor! It was my mother's dream when she was younger.

Now she can afford to feed me AND her baby boy.

Share wealth and technology

Many people believe wealthy, polluting countries should give money to poorer places to help them adapt. New technology could be shared for free too – cutting-edge, climate-friendly technologies are usually made in places with enough money to fund them.

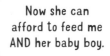

Ooh! Scientists in Japan have found a cure. I hope they send some here.

PLING

Growth

When a country gets wealthier, people often say its economy is growing. **Growth** can lower poverty and keep people healthy, so it can be a good thing. But many people think we need to be careful about *how* we grow economies.

An economy is created when the people in a country make and sell things using the materials they have available, and provide services to each other.

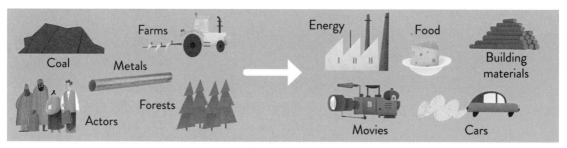

The more people produce, buy and sell, the more the economy grows. *Every* country's economy has grown in the past 150 years – some more than others. Growth has improved living standards enormously, so few people want it to stop.

1919

70% of the world's population lived in poverty.

2019

9% of people lived in poverty.

A happy couple?

In most places, as the economy has grown, so has the amount of energy that a country uses. For over a century, fossil fuels have provided much of that energy. Economists say that growth and fossil fuels have become **coupled**.

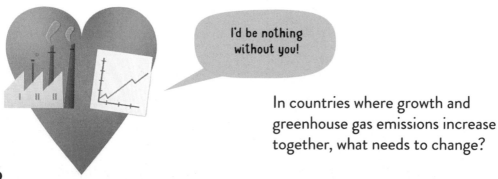

I'd be nothing without you!

In countries where growth and greenhouse gas emissions increase together, what needs to change?

Decoupling

If we're going to protect the planet, some people argue that growth needs to stop. But most studies show that growth *can* continue to rise *while* emissions decrease. This is known as **decoupling** growth from emissions. There are lots of different ideas about how to do it.

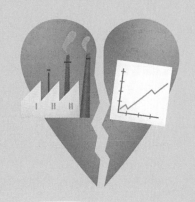

> If we make CLEAN energy CHEAP ENOUGH that people will choose it over fossil fuels, using more energy won't harm the planet as much.

> In rich countries especially, people really like buying NEW STUFF. All that manufacturing emits greenhouse gases. Maybe we need to value simple pleasures more than new possessions?

> We normally measure growth as 'the overall value of everything a country produces, year after year.' What if we change how we measure it?

> If we ALSO measured how happy people are, and how much our money-making damages the planet, maybe we'd get a better picture of whether it's worth it.

As with many ideas in this chapter, there's a big debate about what we do next. The argument about growth is *really* important. The way the world's economies grow will have a big influence on how well we deal with the crisis.

Working together

Despite knowing about global warming for decades, despite all the warnings from scientists, all the definitive data and the damage done, we still can't agree on a plan. Why do we find it so hard to work *together*?

Global emissions have RISEN 50% since countries first agreed to tackle climate change in 1992. To meet the Paris targets, emissions will have to DROP 7% every year until 2030.

Meanwhile, in 2017 the US said that it would leave the Paris Agreement by the end of 2020. Since records began, the US has emitted more greenhouse gas than any other country.

Sharing is hard

The fact is, people are terrible at sharing with each other, even if they understand that it's a good idea.

Time after time, groups of people rapidly use up things that they share. This happens because people act selfishly, without considering how their choices affect everyone else.

Look at the example of traffic jams. To many people, it seems quicker and more convenient to drive to work than to take a bus.

But the more people that choose driving, the less space there is on the road, and the longer the delays.

So everyone ends up worse off, even though they all made a decision that seemed reasonable to them *individually*.

All countries share the climate. Their governments may understand that they *should* cut their emissions. But being selfish is very tempting when they only pay part of the cost (and they worry that others won't play fair). So what can we do?

American economist Elinor Ostrom spent decades studying groups of people who successfully managed to share something without using it all up.

Ostrom's basic lesson was that for collaboration to work, everyone involved needs to know and trust each other and the rules they've agreed together. They need to behave like a close-knit community.

But how can the world be one big community?

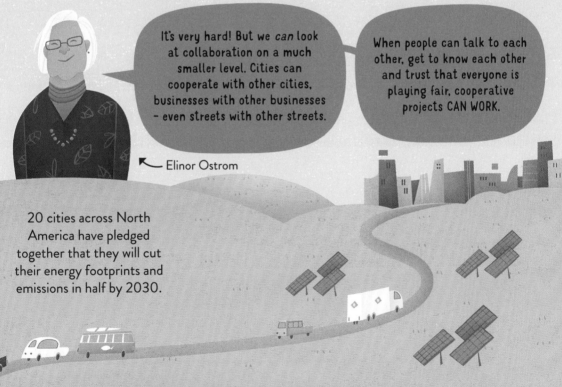

It's very hard! But we *can* look at collaboration on a much smaller level. Cities can cooperate with other cities, businesses with other businesses – even streets with other streets.

When people can talk to each other, get to know each other and trust that everyone is playing fair, cooperative projects CAN WORK.

← Elinor Ostrom

20 cities across North America have pledged together that they will cut their energy footprints and emissions in half by 2030.

If we want to work quickly and effectively, we should start organizing at *every* level of society, and not just rely on governments making the right decisions.

Our brains aren't helping

Psychologists can explain why we struggle to deal with the climate crisis. They've found unhelpful patterns of thinking that lurk in all our brains and make it harder for us to CARE about what's happening.

Our brains are bad at TIME

People tend to prefer short term rewards over long term gains.

Do you want $15 today, or $75 in five years?

$15 now of course!

No matter how big the benefit is, if it's too far in the future, we won't want it. Many of the rewards for dealing with climate change won't be immediate, so it is hard to motivate people to care...

Our brains are too OPTIMISTIC

People overestimate the likelihood of good things happening to them, and underestimate the likelihood of bad things happening.

Should I go out to buy a lottery ticket in this thunderstorm?

Yeah go for it!

You're far more likely to be struck by lightning than you are to win the lottery.

Our brains IGNORE inconvenient facts

No one wants to believe that what *they* do is partly responsible for a global disaster. It's much easier just to ignore it – or deny it.

What? Eating one more hamburger doesn't hurt!

90

Our brains are bad at DISTANCES

If something is far away, it's harder to worry about it.

Oh no! They've stopped running the number 73 bus.

DAILY BUGLE
ARCTIC ICE is nearly GONE!

Global issues don't hit home in the same way that local news does.

Often, warnings about the climate crisis explain that terrible things will happen to polar bears or ice caps. Yet many people in the richest, most polluting countries don't live near these things. It's hard to understand that a problem for a polar bear is also a problem for all of us.

Our brains are bad at BIG numbers

Large numbers don't really speak to us. We struggle to picture what 'millions' of people being forced to migrate or a 'billion' tons of CO_2 actually means.

If people are told about something bad happening to a single named person, they are far more likely to care than if they are told about a large number of people in trouble.

Why are we giving all this money to refugees?

I can't believe TOM HANKS got coronavirus. Poor man.

The 2020 coronavirus pandemic produced an instant global response. But the climate crisis is a huge threat too, and we aren't doing nearly enough to stop it. Being so big, complicated and *relatively* far away, all makes it especially difficult for our brains to grasp its dangers.

Unhelpful habits

Even if people DO recognize the threat of the climate crisis, getting them to change how they behave is a whole new challenge. For instance, if you have a bike, why not start cycling instead of driving?

Sometimes the biggest barrier to change is that you don't have the opportunity.

I *would* cycle to school, but I live by a busy road and it's too dangerous.

But even if you're given an opportunity to change, you may not take it. Often, it's your brain getting in the way again, creating problems known as **psychological barriers**. Here are a few examples.

BRAND NEW CYCLE PATH NOW OPEN!

Cycle to work.
Cycle to school.
Save the planet.

We compare ourselves to others

People are heavily influenced by everyone around them. Like sheep, most of us follow the herd.

My friends aren't cycling to school. I don't want them to think I'm weird?

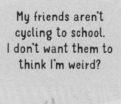

Baaaaah

Change feels risky

Eek, but what if I fall off?

Risks of all kinds – to your health, money, or even what other people think of you – can stop you from changing what you do. You're much less likely to change if there's a chance you might lose something.

We like comfort

Cycle? Nah. Driving is SO much easier.

It's harder to change if it feels inconvenient, or if it feels like too much effort. People with more comfortable lifestyles often find it tough to make sacrifices.

It's hard to break habits...

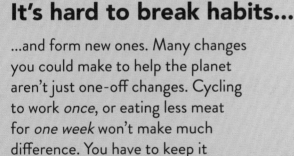

Ah, I give up.

No, don't give up! You can do it!

...and form new ones. Many changes you could make to help the planet aren't just one-off changes. Cycling to work *once*, or eating less meat for *one week* won't make much difference. You have to keep it up for a long time.

If we recognize our psychological barriers, we *can* change our own habits, and find better ways to motivate others. For example, studies show that paying people to recycle is less likely to make it a habit than giving them eye-catching bins. The jazzy bins remind people to *keep* recycling, and so they start doing it every day.

Unintended consequences

Even when people DO take action over the climate crisis, it doesn't always work, and may even make things *worse*.

Here's an example of a good action having unintended, negative consequences. Regina has started bicycling to work, instead of driving.

It's a great decision! Regina saves all this energy by cycling.

But look at all these ways those savings might be wasted...

Regina saves money on fuel. But she chooses to spend this extra money on some new running clothes with a high carbon footprint.

Regina's journey to work is now shorter. She can use the time to take a shower after her cycle. But this uses up energy too.

Feeling pleased about having "done her part" for the climate crisis, Regina allows herself to book a flight to visit her cousin.

Energy savings used up = ¼

Energy savings used up = ⅛

This uses up more than a THOUSAND times the energy she saved to begin with.

When someone makes savings in *one* way, but changes their habits in *other* ways so their savings disappear, it is known as the **rebound effect**.

Here's another example of the rebound effect: despite our machines becoming more *energy efficient*, many people's and businesses' *energy use* keeps growing. Why does that happen?

Machines may consume less energy than before, but that feels like a great reason to use them *more*. When efficiency improvements push down costs – it is tempting to *respend* those savings.

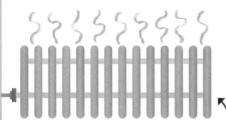

A study in Norway showed that when people installed energy-efficient heating in their homes, they often ended up heating those homes for longer. This got rid of most of the energy savings they'd made.

In Chicago, scientists studied a highrise that switched from old-fashioned lightbulbs to energy-efficient ones. They found that people ended up buying and using lots more of the new kinds of bulbs. Unfortunately, the highrise still used the same amount of energy as before.

Sometimes great efficiency improvements actually make whole countries use up more energy.

When roads are paved, cars burn less fuel. But this in turn makes far-off places seem closer. This means lots of people move out of cities and into sprawling suburbs, a long, energy-sucking drive away from where they work and shop.

But this is terrible! I thought cycling more was a GOOD thing.

It is! And you shouldn't stop – but we have to be very careful to *look after* the savings we've made. We don't want to throw away our gains carelessly.

Different opinions

There are A LOT of different opinions about the climate crisis.
When people can't agree, change becomes slow and difficult. The system
that countries use to solve differences of opinion is called **politics**.

Debate 1: What about all the other problems?

Politicians solve problems by arguing, or **debating**, with each other.
For example: which problem do we fix first?

But Prime Minister, don't
you see how important
carbon taxes are?

I do, but so is education,
health policy, helping
unemployed people and
refugees, and keeping my
citizens safe. Let me sort
those out first.

Debate 2: Well, what should we do about it?

Quite often, when people suggest ways to fix the climate crisis, their solutions
only reflect the things they already think are important.

Some people want
governments to raise taxes
– so that's their solution.

Other people like lower taxes
– and that's how they think the
crisis will be solved.

Other people have very
different priorities.

Tax oil companies so
much they shut down.
That'll end emissions.

That's idiotic! We'll never
get new technologies if we
tax businesses too much.

If we gave animals the
same rights as people,
then we'd treat the
world better.

Debate 3: How can I convince you?

You might think the climate crisis is important and have a clear idea of what to do. But not everyone agrees on the best way to get attention.

Debate 4: Do we even need to help?

Some leaders don't see the need for their country to make changes or sacrifices for the good of the global climate. They *also* don't like being told what to do.

Big money, big profit

It is not just some politicians who seek to profit *now* at the future's expense. It's businesses and people too. For years, some big oil companies denied that the climate crisis was a problem, because doing something about it would cost them money.

As early as the 1950s, some were aware that CO_2 emissions from burning fossil fuels would cause the world to heat up.

Scientists who studied the details discovered how damaging this would be – and how urgent it was that something be done.

Oil companies were making too much money to change their business. Instead they paid for research and advertisements that spread uncertainty and denied that climate change was a problem.

Oil companies also paid money to politicians to help them get elected. When the politicians were in power, they paid them back by opposing laws that tried to reduce fossil fuel use.

Often this isn't illegal – any person or business is allowed to try to persuade governments to do something. This process is known as **lobbying**.

It's too easy to blame just oil companies for this. We are all part of a bigger system that values profits and cheap energy over the planet's future.

> We give people the cheap energy they demand. And we create jobs AND we make a lot of money for a lot of people.

> We give everybody what they tell us they want! It's not OUR responsibility to change that...

Oil companies still make vast profits supplying us with fossil fuels. All that profit counts as economic growth. If you value growth, it's hard to tell those companies to switch to producing clean energy if it means they make less money.

But it doesn't have to be that way. Governments can change incentives, to make it more attractive to leave fossil fuels in the ground, and to make clean energy cheaper.

> Will you vote for me?

> Will you bring in a carbon tax?

In turn, *we* can VOTE for politicians who will make those changes. It doesn't just apply to energy, but to ALL aspects of the economy and the way we live.

That means we have to ask some very big questions. Can we actually change? And, if we do, what do we want to become? What's the best way to run our political system, our economy and our society?

> Those are BIG questions about our fundamental values. I don't even know where to get started...

> It makes my head swim just thinking about it...

How can our values help?

The things we think are important are known as our **values**.
They define the way we treat the planet and each other. Which values
do *you* think we should keep? And which should we change?

OK. How do I work out my values?

Well, one way is to ask yourself some questions. How about this one: if the Earth could speak, what would it say?

Questions like this don't have a right answer. But it's good to start conversations with others and with yourself about what you value most. Here are some other types of questions you might want to think about.

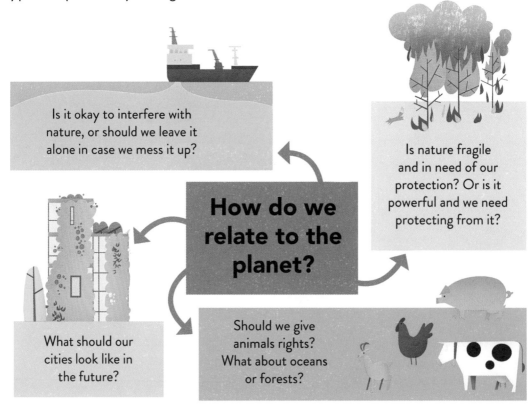

Is it okay to interfere with nature, or should we leave it alone in case we mess it up?

Is nature fragile and in need of our protection? Or is it powerful and we need protecting from it?

How do we relate to the planet?

What should our cities look like in the future?

Should we give animals rights? What about oceans or forests?

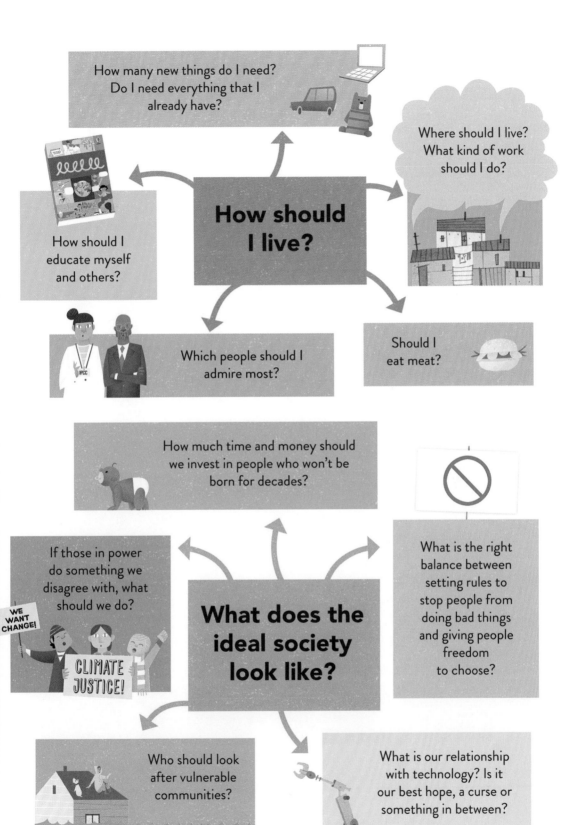

How many new things do I need? Do I need everything that I already have?

Where should I live? What kind of work should I do?

How should I educate myself and others?

How should I live?

Which people should I admire most?

Should I eat meat?

How much time and money should we invest in people who won't be born for decades?

If those in power do something we disagree with, what should we do?

WE WANT CHANGE!

CLIMATE JUSTICE!

What does the ideal society look like?

What is the right balance between setting rules to stop people from doing bad things and giving people freedom to choose?

Who should look after vulnerable communities?

What is our relationship with technology? Is it our best hope, a curse or something in between?

Chapter 5:
What can *I* do?

Now that you've read all about the crisis, you've got a lot of information. But how can you use it? This chapter is here to give YOU the tools to come up with a personal action plan.

Everyone finds change difficult. The first step is to take a deep breath and decide that you want to make a positive change. It's good! It means you are working for a better future for everyone.

OK! So where do we put 1,000 wind turbines?

Achievable goals

Before you start making changes, remember this: there's only so much that ONE person can do. It's important to be kind to yourself and set yourself goals you know you can achieve.

> I'm going to raise taxes on fossil fuel companies and use the money to invest in clean energy!

> Um... full marks for enthusiasm, but you might have to start *smaller*, Ben. Only governments get to raise taxes.

A lot of the solutions that you've seen in this book are BIG, but most people's individual contributions will start small, and stay small. What *you* can do depends on a number of different things.

Your age

This chapter has lots of ideas for things that you can do at almost ANY age.

But there are some things that you can only do once you're old enough.

> I can't vote until I'm 18, but I CAN write a letter to my local politicians with ideas.

And especially when you're younger (and often when you're an adult too) you'll need to ask people's permission or help to do certain things.

> Can I set up a communal garden to grow local vegetables, Dad?

> Yes, but only if I can do it with you.

Where you are

Where do you spend most of your time? That's often a good place to start making a difference.

Let's make a plan for how we can help the planet *from home*.

There are ideas for things you can do at home on the next page.

How much power you have

Some people have jobs that mean they can make big changes to help the planet.

As a politician I actually CAN raise taxes on fossil fuel companies and invest in clean energy!

That was my idea...

So it's the job of people who *don't* have power to persuade those that *do* to act. Many believe that politicians, businesses and community leaders should be held MORE responsible for our climate's future than people with LESS power.

If you're thinking about your future, then aim as big as you like. But there are always small things that you can do NOW.

Got it!

Maybe I'll be able to raise taxes ONE day though...

Helping at home

Here are some achievable changes YOU could suggest to reduce your family's carbon footprint. You might not have the final say on what happens, but there's no harm in making suggestions and doing what you can.

BIG IMPACT choices are...

1. Avoid flying where possible
2. Live as car-free as possible
3. Choose a clean energy provider
4. Eat less meat

Oops!

When you decide to make a change, it's important that you stick to it. Setting clear goals makes this so much easier.

I've decided I'm not going to fly in planes anymore. It's the biggest change I can make to cut my carbon footprint.

Dani's practical tips for cutting down on travel emissions:

- Try to avoid car journeys when trains, buses, cycling or walking are an option.

- Take a staycation – visit your local area.

- Choose nearby vacation destinations.

- Take a train instead of a plane.

- Get your family to switch to an electric car if possible.

I'm only eating meat TWICE a week now. I don't miss it as much as I thought I would: these meat-free burgers are really tasty!

There's no need to give up everything all at once. Set yourself goals that work for you.

A good way to get started is to make up a list of changes you want to make. Here are the lists Dani and Ben put up on their refrigerator:

Eat for the planet

- Remember that 30% of our carbon footprint comes from our diet.

- Eat less meat and dairy.
Look online for alternatives that are produced with fewer emissions.

- Waste less, by composting, not buying too much, and not serving yourself more than you'll eat.

- Try to buy local. Read packaging to find out where your food comes from.

Consume less and appreciate more

- Buy second-hand clothes and books, and give away things you don't want.

- Think about the footprint of anything you buy. Has it come a long way?

- Only buy things you really need. Can you use them more than once? Do you already have something similar?

- Cherish what you have. Enjoy it to the max!

Use less energy

- Do more activities that don't use electricity: read books, play boardgames and have fun outdoors with friends.

- See if your family can switch to LED lights, or insulate your home.

- Turn off lights and turn down the heating. Wear a sweater if it's cold and unplug things at night.

- Wash clothes on lower temperature settings and air dry them instead of tumble drying. Take showers, not baths.

Do things that help the planet and make you feel good

- Plant some trees in your garden and leave it a little wild for the bugs and bees.

- Repair broken things around the house instead of buying new.

- REUSE AND RECYCLE EVERYTHING YOU CAN.

If you start to make changes like these, you will cut your own personal carbon emissions dramatically. There's no time to waste. So why not start making your own list now?

Having a voice

As a young person, you're rarely in charge of how things are run. But there *are* ways to get your voice heard. This is known as **activism**. You can choose to be an activist in lots of different ways.

School strikes

Strikes are when people refuse to do something to prove a point. In 2018, Swedish teenager Greta Thunberg took the bold move to strike from school.

> I skipped school on Fridays to protest outside the Swedish parliament and demand that world leaders do more to help the environment.

> Since then, MILLIONS of people all around the world have skipped school – and work – to protest with me.

ON FRIDAY WE STRIKE!

Local projects

Activism doesn't have to attract global attention to be successful. Starting a project at school or where you live can work too. Take Lesein Mutunkei, a 15 year old from Kenya who combined his love of sports with his passion for forests:

> I made a promise that every time I scored a goal in a match, I'd plant a tree.

> I started off doing it by myself. But people loved it, and I managed to get my school's sports teams to do it too.

> After two years of **Trees4Goals**, we'd planted over 1,200 trees. Goooooal! Could you do the same with your team?

Collect signatures

When you write down what you want to change, then collect signatures to show that LOTS of people want the same thing, it's known as a **petition**. In the UK, Ella and Caitlin McEwan wrote a successful petition in 2019, when they were 9 and 7 years old.

> We noticed that the fast food chains McDonalds and Burger King give plastic toys with some of their meals.

> Plastic is bad for the climate and planet. Making it emits greenhouse gases, and it often ends up in the oceans after we throw it away.

> The petition asked the companies to stop making plastic toys. We posted it online, and over half a million people signed it. Burger King felt the pressure. They've stopped handing out plastic toys with children's meals in the UK.

These examples aren't meant to make you feel like you *have to* become an activist. But they show that, with help and support from friends and adults, change is POSSIBLE. You have other options too...

> I'm writing a letter to my local politician!

Dear Ms. Jackson,

Chigham Forest will be chopped down soon to make space for farms. I know that we need farms, but we also need trees — they're carbon sinks.

I have an idea...

If you're not happy about something where you live, you can write to whoever's in charge, explain what's wrong, and maybe suggest a better idea. This doesn't *always* work, but at least you've forced a person in power to think about it.

Talking about the climate crisis

Talking about the climate crisis is one of the most important things you can do. It's a great way to persuade people to join you in working for a better future. You may pick up useful ideas from them, too.

A good place to start is sharing your plan for reducing your own emissions with your friends and family.

Be happy and positive about the change you are making. Preserving the planet is a joyful thing, especially if you all do it together.

> I want to learn how to fix my own clothes, Grandpa. Will you teach me how to sew?

> You were right about those veggie burgers, Ben. They're delicious!

> Where can I get one?

Don't be shy about telling other people. You might be surprised how many people agree with you.

Better still, your example might inspire them to speak out. Humans are social animals: the more people do something, the more others will join in.

Be careful about the information you share. Make sure it is accurate and up to date. If you exaggerate, it makes it much easier for people who disagree with you to ignore everything you are saying.

When large fires were burning in the Amazon in 2019, a dramatic picture of the rainforest on fire was shared widely on social media. But the picture was of a different fire, in a different year. This mistake allowed people to attack the message and ignore the problem.

If you meet someone who doesn't agree with you about the climate crisis, it may not work to argue with them or throw lots of facts in their faces. People can become angry if you directly challenge their opinion, which makes them very unlikely to listen. Here's a strategy that can lead to more productive conversations. It was developed by Smart Politics, a research group from the US.

1. Ask

The climate crisis is NONSENSE! The Earth isn't getting hotter.

Instead of challenging people you disagree with, ask genuine, curious questions so you understand them better and they feel respected.

That's interesting, can you tell me more about that?

2. Listen

Sure. Did you know there are LOTS of scientists who say it's all exaggerated.

Listen to what they say and ask follow-up questions.

And you have your doubts too. How has the weather been near you?

3. Reflect

No warming at all! The last two winters have been the coldest I've known.

Show you understand them by summarizing what they've told you, and how they feel.

Right, and you don't feel those changes have anything to do with the climate crisis.

4. Agree

Yeah – and even if the climate is changing, it's nothing to do with what humans are doing.

Pick something you both agree on and talk about that.

I agree that the climate changes naturally. It's always done that...

5. Share

Maybe there have been *some* changes, but those protestors go way too far.

Share how you think by telling them a story about a personal experience. Hopefully, they will now listen to you...

You know, the thing that first got me interested in all this was...

Who can I trust?

Conversations about the climate crisis in the news, online and even in person, can be bewildering. There's SO much information out there. It's difficult to tell what's true and what's not.

Think like a scientist – be critical

The solution, whenever you look at ANY information, is to ask the same kinds of questions that an IPCC scientist would.

Oh no! This article says that a billion people are going to die of heatstroke by 2050.

That's awful! But is it really true?

Is the information up to date? When was it published?

Is the author an expert in this particular topic? If not, they might have made an error.

If you have doubts about a fact, here are some useful questions you can ask about it.

Does the author provide references to show where their facts come from? If they don't, they might be making them up.

Does the author make it clear what they don't know or are uncertain about? Too much certainty, especially when talking about the future, is a bad sign.

Check the references – are the quotes being used in the right context?

Do other experts in this subject agree with this information? Have they had the same results?

Are you reassured that the information *is* accurate? If you aren't, you might like to investigate further.

Think about how and why this particular fact was chosen. What motivated the author to tell you this?

You might be able to find out who paid for the research. Are *they* trying to push a particular point of view?

Can I trust *myself*?

Remember that your opinions and the things YOU think are important make you more likely to believe some facts more than others. So keep an open mind. Don't always believe people you agree with and dismiss people you don't.

Just because you like the way someone thinks, it doesn't mean they are right. Challenge yourself to listen respectfully to people you disagree with.

Too much information

It is unhealthy to spend too much time reading, listening and worrying about the climate crisis. Especially with the internet, people have constant access to information. But that doesn't mean you have to pay attention all the time.

A healthy head

Often, people worry or feel sad and angry about the crisis. Those feelings are normal, but they're not very pleasant. As you learn and think more about it, keep an eye on how you feel. It's important to stay healthy.

Here are some negative thoughts people have quite often, and some positive ideas to help you deal with them.

I'm sad and overwhelmed. There are SO many terrible things happening to the planet.

I'm terrified. Humans are going to become extinct, aren't we?

It's true, there are. But so many good things are happening too. Right now many people are working hard to fix the climate. And we've managed to fix other environmental problems in the past, such as acid rain.

No we aren't! We have the tools we need to survive. The crisis will put lots of people at risk, but almost all experts think extinction is extremely, extremely unlikely.

CLIMA JUSTI

This is hopeless. I've been cycling to school and not wasting food, but the crisis is still happening.

I feel guilty. I'm not doing enough.

It's frustrating, but ONE person's actions at home aren't going to change the whole world. Your actions are still important though, because it's a GROUP effort. As more people change, so will the climate - so keep it up!

There's only so much YOU can do. Forcing yourself to do more can distract you from the fact that people with POWER are the ones who can make the BIGGEST difference.

Looking after yourself

When you feel worried, sad or angry, there are ways to make those feelings shrink or disappear – much like healing a wound. Psychologists call these useful fixes **coping strategies**.

Ben worries a lot about the crisis. You might too. As a coping strategy, you could...

...turn your thoughts into actions

This can mean two things. Activities that you enjoy, and that have nothing to do with the crisis, make excellent distractions from unwelcome thoughts.

Alternatively, you could turn your worries into positive actions. Try to do something that helps the planet. This might make you feel more in control.

...be mindful

When you have lots of thoughts in your head, it's easy to stop noticing what's around you. Being **mindful** means finding an activity that helps you focus on the here and now.* It might sound odd, but moving your focus to the present moment can release calm, relaxing chemicals into your brain.

...talk

Talking to your family and friends about how you feel means you don't have to deal with your feelings on your own.

Oh poor you, Ben. I know that feeling. It's not nice. Join us in the garden, we'll cheer you up.

#sigh

If you feel worried a lot of the time, talk to a grown-up you trust. They might be able to suggest ways to make the worries feel manageable.

*You can find some ideas for mindful activities on Usborne Quicklinks.

What's holding you back?

If you're ever struggling to do something, you can use the questions and information on this page to help you work out what's getting in your way. Then, turn the page to discover how to overcome it.

Psychologists have identified THREE main types of BARRIERS that stop people from engaging in new activities.

When you don't have the necessary skills or abilities, it's called a **CAPABILITY BARRIER.** It might be your brain getting in the way...

...or it might be your body.

Do you keep forgetting to do it, or how to do it?

Are you not strong enough to lift something?

Do you know how to do it?

Are you injured or feeling ill?

Are you too short to reach something?

Do you find it hard to concentrate?

Are you allergic to something?

Do you find it hard to make decisions?

Hmm... I can't choose what kind of tree to plant.

If I walk or cycle to work it makes my hayfever worse. SNIFF.

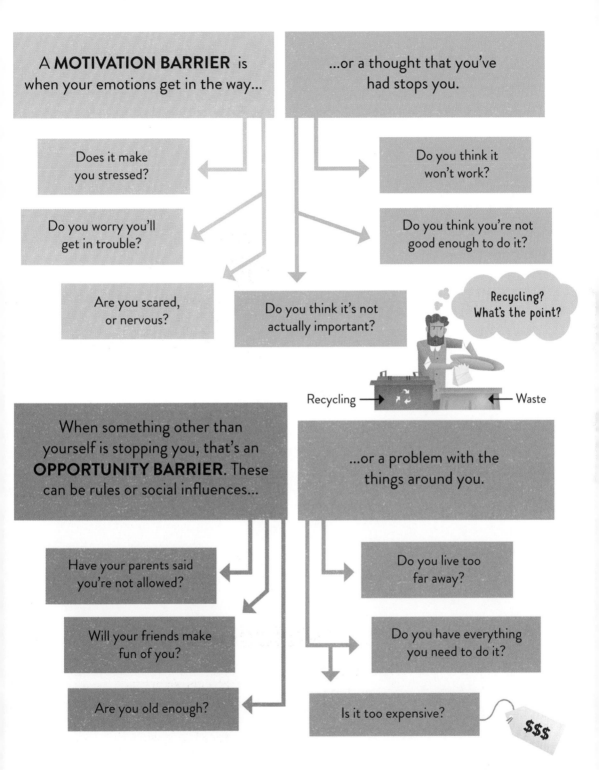

It's often a MIX of barriers that holds a person back. For example, with Enofe's hayfever you could say that his allergy is the problem (a capability barrier), or the pollen is the problem (an opportunity barrier). Finding a way around either problem would make walking to work much easier for him.

Breaking down barriers

Once you've identified what's stopping you from doing something, see if any of these tricks can help you. Different tricks work better for different people, and for different barriers.

Educate yourself

If you don't know how to do something, you could learn how and keep trying until you feel confident.

And that's how you sew on a button!

Reward yourself

A treat or reward for doing something can give you the motivation to start or keep going. It might even feel like a game rather than a chore.

I'll treat myself to a chocolate chip cookie IF I finish reading this scientific research.

REPORT

Give yourself restrictions

Set yourself rules you have to stick to that stop you from doing something too much. Starting with small rules is easier.

I'll fly MAXIMUM once this year. If I fly more than that, then it's ZERO flights next year.

Find a role model

If you find somebody you aspire to be or something you want to copy, that gives you a target to aim for.

> Oh wow! I want our garden to look like that one.

Change things around you

Look around your house – is anything stopping you from making the changes you want to make? Can you fix it?

> Our new compost bin is great! We don't waste ANY food anymore.

Find help and support

There's no shame in getting help. It can come from a *person*...

...or a *thing*.

> You can do it, Ben! Test out your speech on us.

shake

shake

shake

> These allergy meds made my hayfever pretty much disappear!

Don't worry if these don't work. Sometimes, barriers are TOO big to beat, and that's okay. But it's worth giving these tricks a try to find that out for yourself.

Lessons from another crisis

The climate crisis is not the only challenge the world has faced recently. What do experts think we can learn from the coronavirus pandemic of 2020?

Lesson 1: We *can* actually make big changes...

When the threat seemed dangerous enough, people and governments responded rapidly, and changed their lifestyles enormously. In some ways this is encouraging for the climate crisis – it shows big change is possible.

At the start of 2020 I shut down THE WORLD.

To stop the virus from spreading, 9 in 10 people globally faced travel restrictions. Almost ALL travel ground to a halt.

Schools shut, workplaces closed and many people stayed at home for *months*.

...but will that be enough?

The 2020 lockdown caused a big drop in travel emissions as people stayed home. This sounds good, but it is also worrying, because it didn't lower emissions by *that* much. Emissions rose quickly again as countries opened up.

Just flying and driving less won't be enough to keep emissions falling.

IPCC

That means BIG structural changes will be just as important – particularly to how we get our energy.

Lesson 2: Prepare better for uncertainty

Many experts predicted that a pandemic was certain to happen. They just didn't know when it would come. Might we have done better if we'd prepared more in advance? Why do we find it difficult to plan ahead for disaster?

Our plans for the future need to be designed so they are FLEXIBLE enough to cope with surprises. The climate crisis will be full of them.

No one wants to think about what will happen if the permafrost melts too much. But we need to have a plan in case it does...

Lesson 3: A glimpse of an alternative future

The start of the coronavirus pandemic was a terrible, traumatic experience for millions of people. But the sudden change it forced on society gave us a vision of how the world might look if things were different.

Car-free cities are cleaner and nicer to live in.

I never thought that people would help each other as much as they have.

What changes did YOU notice that you hope will stick?

What happens next?

Now that you've read this book, you've got the tools to imagine the future that YOU want and an idea of how to start your journey towards it.

The climate crisis is real. It is already changing the world around us.

It will be part of our future. But *how big* a part is still up to us.

It is not going to be easy. There is no magic solution that will make the climate crisis go away. Instead there are MANY things we need to fix.

Dad looks so happy. I'm glad we're doing this together.

The good news is that we know what we need to do and we have the tools and expertise we need to do it, together.

COMMUNITY GARDEN GRAND OPENING PARTY!

But will we change?

The future belongs to young people.

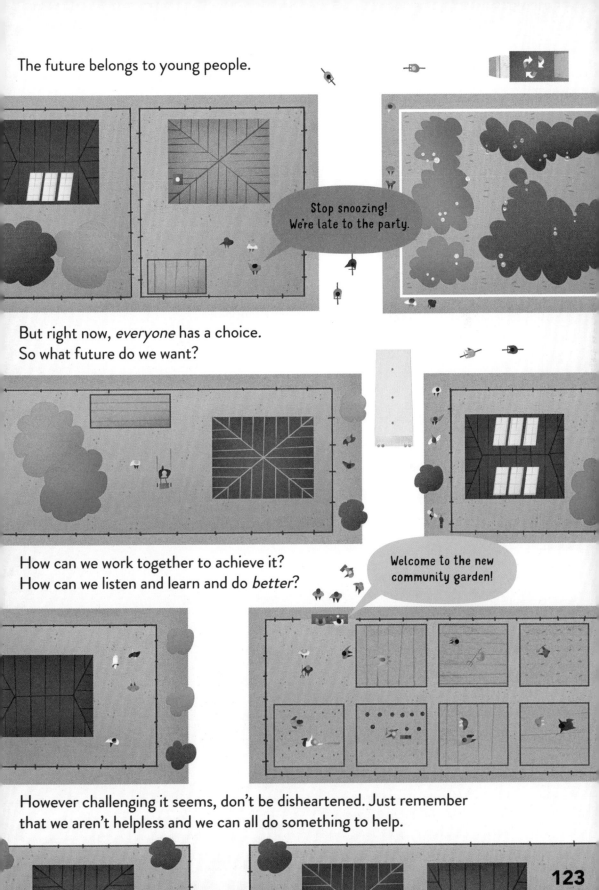

But right now, *everyone* has a choice.
So what future do we want?

How can we work together to achieve it?
How can we listen and learn and do *better*?

However challenging it seems, don't be disheartened. Just remember
that we aren't helpless and we can all do something to help.

We *must* protect the planet.

It is beautiful
and unique.

ON FRIDAY
WE STRIKE!

It's our only home.

Glossary

This glossary explains some of the words used in this book.
Words written in *italic* type are explained in other entries.

adaptation a change that makes you better suited to your environment.

albedo the reflectiveness of Earth.

atmosphere the blanket of gases that surrounds Earth.

carbon a chemical element found in all living things.

carbon dioxide (CO₂) a *greenhouse gas* that is emitted by burning fossil fuels, trees and plants.

carbon capture any system that removes *greenhouse gases* from the *atmosphere*, or stops them from entering.

carbon neutral any system that, overall, absorbs as much *carbon dioxide* as it emits.

carbon sinks any system that absorbs and stores *carbon*.

climate what we expect the weather to be like in the long term.

climate justice making sure vulnerable and disadvantaged people are looked after and included in efforts to deal with the crisis.

crisis a time when a difficult or important decision must be made.

economy, the how people in a community or across the world make, buy and sell things to each other.

economic growth when people in a country make, buy and sell more and more things.

emissions *greenhouse gases* given off by lots of different processes, such as burning fossil fuels.

fossil fuels coal, oil and gas, formed from the fossils of long dead plants and animals, burned for use as fuel.

glaciers rivers of ice found in polar regions and on some mountains.

global heating an increase in average temperatures across the whole planet.

greenhouse effect, the the way that gases in the *atmosphere* trap heat.

greenhouse gas any gas in the *atmosphere* that keeps Earth warm.

incentives anything that encourages people to make a particular choice.

IPCC, the the Intergovernmental Panel on Climate Change, responsible for assessing the science related to climate change and suggesting options.

mitigation actions taken to try to reduce the effects of the climate crisis, mainly by reducing emissions.

natural disasters events that happen outside of human control, such as earthquakes or wildfires.

Paris Agreement, the an agreement made by almost every country in the world in 2015 to keep global heating to well below 2°C.

pollution anything that human activity puts into the air, oceans or land that harms living things.

weather the state of the atmosphere (e.g. temperature, wind, rain) at a particular place and time.

Index

Acknowledgments

Written by
Andy Prentice and Eddie Reynolds

Illustrated by
Borja Ramón López Cotelo,
trading as El Primo Ramón

Edited by
Alex Frith

Designed by
Jamie Ball and Freya Harrison

Series editor: Jane Chisholm
American editor: Carrie Armstrong

Series designer:
Stephen Moncrieff

Climate Change consultants:
Dr. Steve Smith,
University of Oxford
Dr. Ajay Gambhir,
Imperial College, London

Additional cover art:
Stephen Collins

With thanks to
Jake Reynolds for his help and advice,
Professor Ed Hawkins (University of Reading)
http://www.showyourstripes.info
Professor Richard Betts MBE (University of Exeter),
Dr. Rhian Rees-Owen and Dr. Sam Bradley